Tragedy: A Very Short Introduction

VERY SHORT INTRODUCTIONS are for anyone wanting a stimulating and accessible way in to a new subject. They are written by experts, and have been published in more than 25 languages worldwide.

The series began in 1995, and now represents a wide variety of topics in history, philosophy, religion, science, and the humanities. Over the next few years it will grow to a library of around 200 volumes – a Very Short Introduction to everything from ancient Egypt and Indian philosophy to conceptual art and cosmology.

Very Short Introductions available now:

For more information visit our web site

www.oup.co.uk/vsi/

Adrian Poole

TRAGEDY

A Very Short Introduction

OXFORD

UNIVERSITY PRESS

OXFORD
UNIVERSITY PRESS

Great Clarendon Street, Oxford OX2 6DP

Oxford University Press is a department of the University of Oxford.
It furthers the University's objective of excellence in research, scholarship,
and education by publishing worldwide in

Oxford New York

Auckland Cape Town Dar es Salaam Hong Kong Karachi
Kuala Lumpur Madrid Melbourne Mexico City Nairobi
New Delhi Shanghai Taipei Toronto

With offices in

Argentina Austria Brazil Chile Czech Republic France Greece
Guatemala Hungary Italy Japan Poland Portugal Singapore
South Korea Switzerland Thailand Turkey Ukraine Vietnam

Oxford is a registered trade mark of Oxford University Press
in the UK and in certain other countries

Published in the United States
by Oxford University Press Inc., New York

British Library Cataloguing in Publication Data

Data available

Library of Congress Cataloging in Publication Data

Data available

ISBN 978-0-19-280235-4

5 7 9 10 8 6 4

Typeset by RefineCatch Ltd, Bungay, Suffolk
Printed in Great Britain by
Ashford Colour Press Ltd, Gosport, Hampshire

Contents

Acknowledgements

I owe a debt to the numerous students and colleagues with whom I have discussed tragedy over many years at Cambridge. I am also grateful for recent specific advice and suggestions to Anne Barton, Jonathan Bate, Ian Donaldson, Robert Douglas-Fairhurst, Kelvin Everest, Tamara Follini, Gérald Garutti, Simon James, Jessica Martin, Drew Milne, and most of all to Margaret de Vaux. I must thank George Miller for the original invitation to contribute this volume to the series, Emily Jolliffe, Becky O'Connor, and Emma Simmons for their assistance and encouragement en route, and my editors Marsha Filion and James Thompson for seeing the work through its final stages. I am gratefully conscious of the generous support I have enjoyed from the award of a British Academy Readership for a larger project on witnessing tragedy, without which this short book would have been even longer in reaching completion.

List of illustrations

The publisher and the author apologize for any errors or omissions in the above list. If contacted they will be pleased to rectify these at the earliest opportunity.

Introduction

Tragedy is a precious word. We use it to confer dignity and value on
violence, catastrophe, agony, and bereavement. 'Tragedy' claims that
this death is exceptional. Yet these supposedly special fatalities are
in our ears and eyes every day, on the roads, in the skies, out there in
foreign lands and right here at home, the latest bad news. Is the
word now bandied around so freely that it has lost all meaning? Do
our conceptions of tragedy have any real connection with those of
the ancient Greeks, with whom it originated two and half thousand
years ago as the description of a particular kind of drama? How did
tragedy migrate from the Greeks to Shakespeare and Racine, from
drama to other art forms, from fiction to real events? What needs
has the idea of tragedy served, and to what use and abuse has it
been put?

This *Very Short Introduction* addresses these questions through a
series of nine topics. Chapter 1 considers the distance between our
modern application of the words 'tragic' and 'tragedy' and their
origins in 5th-century Athens, including some changing ideas about
fate and accident, the importance of stories and plots, and the
significance of the disagreement between Plato and Aristotle over
tragedy's claims to truth and its effects on those who witness it. In
Chapter 2 we will look at the possibility that tragedy as a living art
form belongs to the past, to ages when artists and audiences drew
on shared religious beliefs, including beliefs about the meaning of

pain and punishment. Chapter 3 suggests that tragedy is an art particularly concerned with our need to lay the past to rest and the dangers of failing to do so; hence tragedy's interest in ghosts and revenge, in mourning and memory, in the ambivalent models provided by 'heroes'. In Chapter 4 we turn our attention to the questions of blame, responsibility, and guilt, to Aristotle's notion of 'error' and to the process of scapegoating. Chapter 5 describes some of the big ideas about tragedy that theorists, including the influential figures of Hegel and Nietzsche, have developed over the last two hundred years, and the resistance or outright hostility such ideas have provoked by their contempt for the reality of pain. Chapter 6 affords some relief by raising the question of comedy in tragedy, especially the role of scornful laughter, both for characters within the fiction and for audiences and readers outside it. In Chapter 7 we consider the importance to tragedy of verbal eloquence and its frustration; the reticence, stammering, and silence to which human beings may be reduced and out of which they can seek to break. Chapter 8 focuses on the different kinds of time that tragedies bring together: the experience of waiting 'between times' and the moment of decisive action when what's done is done, conjunctions of past and future in the here and now that the visual arts are well placed to capture. In conclusion, Chapter 9 turns to the problem of endings in tragedy, and the complex desires for justice and truth that they excite in those who witness it.

Who needs tragedy? Can we imagine a world without tragedy? Would we want to? These are some of the tough questions that the art of tragedy puts into words and images, so tellingly – at least in the hands of its greatest exponents – that it seems we can't do without it.

Chapter 1
Who needs it?

Bad news

Open the paper, turn on the news, and sooner or later you'll meet the words 'tragic' and 'tragedy'. Even as I write, 19 Chinese cockle-pickers are reported drowned in Morecambe Bay, Lancashire. 'The gangs behind the tragedy are on the run', one headline assures us. The story attracts no fewer than ten more 'tragedies' across two reports and a leader in the *Guardian* (7 February 2004). Tragedy: how many more times, of how many more disasters, before you read *this*? Even as this goes to press, the number of lives lost to the Asian tsunami and its aftermath appears literally countless.

It's easy to feel overwhelmed by the word. Once it meant something special, as it did to John Milton, writing in the middle of the 17th century:

> Sometime let gorgeous Tragedy
> In sceptred pall come sweeping by,
> Presenting Thebes, or Pelops' line,
> Or the tale of Troy divine.
> Or what (though rare) of later age,
> Ennobled hath the buskined stage.

He is thinking of Tragedy as a regal figure from ancient Greece, like Oedipus (from Thebes) and Agamemnon (descendant of Pelops) and the heroes from Homer's *Iliad* (the tale of Troy), and he dresses them up with lofty old words like 'pall' (robe) and 'buskin' (the high thick-soled boot supposedly worn by the actors in Athenian tragedy). It's a long way from the tale of those Chinese cockle-pickers. Nothing gorgeous about *them*. No sceptred palls or buskins in evidence, no connection with ancient myth, and not much chance of dramatic ennobling. For Milton, tragedy was not something that happens every day. It was an idea attached to a specific form of drama performed at special times and places, at the religious festivals of ancient Athens and the courts of modern kings and noblemen.

Though its origins are shrouded in obscurity, 'tragedy' first emerged into the light in Athens around 533 BC with the actor Thespis (from whom we get 'thespian'). It enjoyed a long high noon through the following century, from which a handful of masterpieces have survived in their entirety, seven attributed to Aeschylus, seven to Sophocles, and 19 to Euripides, the great trio of playwrights of whom we shall hear more throughout this book. We have fragments, titles, and reports of many more – Sophocles alone is said to have composed 130 – and it's sobering to realize what a small fraction has come down to us. The honour of having their work performed at the Festival of the Great Dionysia was restricted to three dramatists selected to compete for the prize of 'best tragic poet'. Each had to supply three tragedies and a satyr play, a grotesquely comic after-piece featuring a chorus of satyrs (half-man and half-beast), of which only one complete example, the *Cyclops* of Euripides, has survived. There were other competitions for comedy and dithyramb (a form of choral song).

Special occasions, special people: tragedy portrayed the fate of famous men and women – legends such as Oedipus and Medea – in elevated style and language. Not of nobodies like you or me, let alone Chinese cockle-pickers, who could have hoped at best for a walk-on part as slaves or messengers. Yet before we succumb to nostalgia, we should note that Milton himself had to defend tragedy from 'the small esteem, or rather infamy' into which it had fallen in his day. Like other neoclassical writers, Milton deplored the way modern authors had mixed up tragedy and comedy together, 'introducing trivial and vulgar persons' as he put it, or as Sir Philip Sidney before him, 'mingling kings and clowns'. Tragedy has always been precious and precarious, as if something dangerous might invade it or escape from it. Better keep out the clowns – the trivial and the vulgar.

There's still the small matter of the goat. The word 'tragedy' seems to be derived from two Greek words, for 'goat' and 'song'. Nobody quite knows why. Was the goat once a prize? Does it have something to do with the chorus of satyrs out of which Aristotle suggests that tragedy evolved? Later commentators thought the goat expressed a truth about the fall of great men, who look good to begin with but end up badly. Just like a goat, said Francesco da Buti in 1395, who has 'a prince-like look in the front (horns and beard) but a rear end that is filthy and naked', and Giovanni da Serravalle a few years later, going one better: 'for a goat has a beautiful aspect, but when it passes it gives off a mighty stink from its tailquarters'.

Whatever its origins, Greek tragedy sports few conspicuous goats. Yet the satyr play followed close on its heels, and in plays like Euripides' *Bacchae* the bestial world presses hard on the human. As the human is always menaced by relapse into the animal, so the purity of tragedy as a genre is always under threat from its 'inferiors'. An alternative to the protectionism of a Milton or a Sidney would be to let the riff-raff in and let tragedy out of its fortress-prison. There are premonitions of this in Shakespeare's mingling of kings and clowns, and supportive precedent in the idea of 'tragicomedy' first announced by the Roman comic dramatist Plautus in the preface to his *Amphitruo* (c. 195 BC), and developed by Italian theorists and dramatists in the 16th century. But it is only in the last couple of hundred years that the idea that *anyone* can be the subject of tragedy has really taken hold. 'Tragedy' has not lost all meaning. The word still ennobles, connoting prestige and conferring dignity. It claims that this catastrophe is exceptional, the matter of headlines. But how long do the headlines last? And now, unless there are pictures, it's barely news at all (see Figure 1). This makes one reflect on the tragedies still waiting to be heard and read and caught on tape – and on those that never will be.

"Adding to the tragedy was the fact that no one caught it on tape for your amusement."

1. Attention deficit

Accidents

Two people interviewed about the deaths of the Chinese cockle-pickers independently remarked that, 'This was a tragedy waiting to happen'. An interesting variation on the paradox of 'an accident waiting to happen', this suggests how closely our notions of tragedy are bound up with ideas about accident. 'Tragedy' may connote inevitability and 'accident' chance, yet somehow they are embroiled with each other. If an accident is entirely unexpected, then it might be thought unavoidable, but if it is *waiting* to happen, then surely it can be foreseen and prevented. (Oedipus would not have agreed, after all the pains that he took proved unavailing.) The *Guardian* leader on the Morecambe Bay tragedy suggests the other side of the paradox. Reflecting on 'the sinuous, hidden paths which draw underpaid workers into such lethal occupations', the writer concludes that, 'It takes a tragedy to open a sudden, surprising window.' This is a good description of the best investigative journalism. It is also remarkably close to Aristotle's description of the plots best designed to excite pity and terror, 'emotions most likely to be stirred when things happen unexpectedly but because of each other': that is, plots that are both surprising and logical.

Over the last two hundred years, tragedy has been liberated from the realm of art but it has not abandoned it. Of the many forces at work, the development of the modern media that disseminate what we call 'the news' is obviously a crucial one. The news brings tragedy home to us. Most notably in the way it raises the question of 'tragic accidents', as it does, for example, in an engraving from a French newspaper of 1895 (Figure 2). This momentarily ennobles M. Harry Alis, though it does not tell us the name of the opponent who killed him, nor the names of their seconds. Nor does it tell us how much of a surprise it came to the two duellists that one of them ended up dead. Shouldn't you expect to kill or be killed in a duel like this? But not all duels end tragically.

Our modern notions of accident can be compared with older ideas of Chance, Fortune, and Fate. In medieval thought the Wheel of Fortune offered an apparently reassuring image of inevitability, as long as you viewed it from the proper distance and perspective. You could see that what goes up was fated to come down. In a 15th-century illustration from Jean de Meun's translation of Boethius' *Consolation of Philosophy* (Figure 3), the regal figure of Fortune seems to be instructing Boethius in the meaning of her Wheel. He is, we could say, the Philosophical

UN DUEL TRAGIQUE.— MORT DE M. HARRY ALIS

2. Famous for fifteen minutes, or less

Spectator. He partly corresponds to the chorus in ancient Greek tragedy, but also to the more individualized figures we meet in Renaissance and modern tragedy, such as Titian's King Midas in 'The Flaying of Marsyas' (see p. 68 and Figure 10), or the lawyer Alfieri in Arthur Miller's *A View from the Bridge* (1955). Must the Philosophical Spectator climb on to Fortune's Wheel or can he avoid it? Is this the question he is asking Fortune, or one of them? Is Fortune really as predictable as this image of her Wheel suggests?

Compare with this another figure of female fatality with a different kind of wheels: the funny skeleton in the feathered hat and scarf on the rampage in her lethal motor-car (Figure 4). Not quite so funny when you realize the cartoon is making a serious point about 'unlicensed drivers', while taking an underhand shot at women drivers, and indeed all women on the loose. Not funny at all when we think of all the men, women, and children killed on the roads

8

3. Fatality: an old idea

every day in 'tragic accidents', few of them as gorgeous as Princess Diana.

Fortune, Chance, Accident: the medieval figure is as serene as the modern is turbulent. It may be that the raging ghoul comes closer than the courteous queen to our sense of fatality now. Yet each expresses one aspect of the conflict that tragedy provokes. It was inevitable, it should never have happened; it could have been predicted, it was a bolt from the blue. We might compare two personifications, the statue of Melpomene, the Tragic Muse, from the early part of the 5th century BC (Figure 5), and the drawing of *Tragoedie* by Gustav Klimt, from 1897 (Figure 6). The ancient face is tranquil, candid, wise. The modern is a mask as well as a face: the

9

4. Fatality: a modern version

effect is at once seductive and repellent, controlled and abandoned. Melpomene seems permanent, Tragoedie fugitive; one inspires trust, the other suspicion. One derives from a great ancient city, the Athens of Sophocles; the other from a great modern city, one of the crucibles of what we call 'modernism', the Vienna of Sigmund Freud and others. But each expresses an aspect of what we want – or need – from tragedy.

5. **Tragic Muse (ancient)**

TRAGOEDIE

6. Tragic Muse (modern)

Life goes on

News headlines fade and so does our sense of the tragedy in real lives and deaths. 'Tragedy' is the cry we now hear when the news first breaks. Why? Because we don't yet know enough, especially about who or what is to blame – though we certainly want to. We don't yet know enough about the past, nor do we know how the story will develop as the investigations proceed. As the shocking event becomes absorbed into something called history, the analyses,

12

explanations, and counter-explanations proliferate. The raw emotions cool. The tears dry. The flowers wither. In a year's time or two, we may wonder why so many people got so distressed.

Others may barely even have noticed. W. H. Auden makes a fine poem out of a painting by Pieter Brueghel about the death of Icarus, the boy who flew too near the sun and fell to a watery death. All Brueghel lets us see of him is his white legs disappearing into the sea. Who cares? No one inside the painting.

> the ploughman may
> Have heard the splash, the forsaken cry,
> But for him it was not an important failure; . . .
> . . . and the expensive delicate ship that must have seen
> Something amazing, a boy falling out of the sky,
> Had somewhere to get to and sailed calmly on.

People have work to do, their living to make, their lives to get on with.

When Shakespeare's Octavius Caesar receives news of his rival Mark Antony's death, his first reaction is disappointment:

> The breaking of so great a thing should make
> A greater crack. The rivèd world
> Should have shook lions into civil streets,
> And citizens to their dens.

(*Antony and Cleopatra*, V. i. 14–17)

It's a bit of a let-down. Antony and Cleopatra recede smoothly into the legends they've been dying to become; the future Emperor Augustus advances into his. What about all the others, the nobodies who have gone missing in the course of the play? They enjoy no such luck, apart from an honourable mention from Antony's wife and Caesar's sister, Octavia, who predicts that 'Wars 'twixt you twain would be / As if the world should cleave, and that slain men /

Should solder up the rift' (III. iv. 30–2). Life does not go on for *them*. Nor do they pass into legend. These mass unmarked graves haunt the modern sense of tragedy. They challenge the old idea that tragedy, if it's to deserve its name, ought to be at once spectacular *and* enduring. Like a work of art.

So has 'tragedy' decisively migrated from the realm of art to real life? Not exactly. There's nothing new about seeing tragedy in real events or making tragedy out of them. We don't know who wrote the Latin tragedy *Octavia* about the wife Nero had murdered in AD 63, but he wisely waited until the Emperor had killed himself five years later. The historian Cassius Dio (c. AD 150–235) was writing from a safer distance when he described as a tragedy Nero's murder of his unspeakable mother Agrippina in AD 59. This suggests the ease with which the term could be applied to a real event without elaborating it into artistic form, either in drama or narrative. Christian writers were ready to get in on this act. Both the martyrdom of St Romanus and the incarnation of Christ were called 'great tragedies'. And we can find more secular examples again in the Middle Ages, such as the drowning in 1120 of Prince William, grandson of the Conqueror, and the Peasants' Revolt near the end of the 14th century.

'All the world's a stage', as Shakespeare's Jaques famously has it (*As You Like It*, II. vii. 139). The idea that the world is a theatre and Fortune its dramatist can be traced back a long way. Famous historical figures whose stories could be interpreted in the Middle Ages as tragedy included Alexander, Julius Caesar, and Croesus. These are the last three examples cited by Chaucer's Monk in his tale of the Fall of Great Men (which begins with the rather less historical figures of Lucifer, Adam, Sampson, and Hercules). That's simply what tragedy is: 'The harm of hem that stoode in heigh degree, / And fillen [fell] so that ther nas no remedie / To brynge hem out of hir adversitee'. Shakespeare would draw more complicated inferences about the role of Fortune in human affairs from his reading of history, both English and Roman, in Holinshed and Plutarch. Perhaps Fortune is not the only artist composing our lives as tragedies. We can take a hand in it ourselves, like the Emperor Nero or Antonin Artaud, heir to the Romantic tradition of the *poète maudit* and godfather to the modern 'Theatre of Cruelty'. In 1935 Artaud announced that tragedy on stage was no longer enough for him and that now he was going to live it out for real: *'La tragèdie sur la scène ne me suffit plus. Je vais la transporter dans ma vie.'*

'Real life' does not speak for itself. It has to be turned into words, stories, and plots. It is only when these are lifted out of the unstoppable flow that they hold our protracted attention. Where tragedy's concerned, there is no absolute reason why they have to be told in the form of drama, performed in a theatre. This is why Aristotle is right to insist that the poet's business is to make plots (*mythoi*) not verses. That's what we need from tragedy, he says: good plots.

History

So the daily news is one thing, with its instant exclamations and snap judgements. ('Anger at paparazzi who caused crash' was one prematurely confident headline, 24 hours after the death of Diana.) There's another kind of story-telling that has a more tenacious purchase on the idea of tragedy. The roots of 'history' lie in the ancient Greek word for 'inquiry'. Over the last 50 years many books have announced the result of their inquiries under the rubric of tragedy: The Tragedy of Afghanistan, Africa, Algeria, Austria, Cambodia, Central Europe, Chile, Europe, Greece, Kashmir, Lebanon, Nazi Germany, Palestine, Paraguay, Russia, and Yugoslavia. Not to mention Iraq. By the time you read this, there will have been more such. The lives of historical characters have also attracted the title of 'tragedy': Mary Queen of Scots, King Charles I, John Ruskin, Trotsky, Gandhi, Ramsay MacDonald, Winston Churchill, the Kennedy family, Lyndon Johnson, and Ken Saro-Wiwa. We can add to this the association of tragedy with the death of particular individuals and the countries they represent, such as Ireland or Northern Ireland, from the *Phoenix Park Murders: Conflict, Compromise and Tragedy in Ireland, 1879–1882* by Tom Corfe (1968) to *Bobby Sands and the Tragedy of Northern Ireland* by John M. Feehan (1983). You can find books on *The Tragedy of Knighthood* (1979), *The Tragedy of Labour* (1980), and *The Tragedy of the Nigerian Socialist Movement* (1980). You can even find *The Tragedy of the Salmon: The Scottish Fishery and the 1986 Salmon Act* (1995).

Since 1800 tragedy has provided a familiar way of reading history – not all history but certain exemplary stories within it, such as those which tell the rise and fall of political leaders from Napoleon onwards, or the fate of ambitious political movements, especially those aimed at radical or revolutionary change. Where these involve signal loss of life, tragedy and history seem fused together. Something like this came close to happening in the late 5th century BC when Thucydides was writing his *History of the Peloponnesian War* (431–404 BC) as Euripides was producing his great tragedies of war, *Hecuba* (c. 424 BC) and *Trojan Women* (415 BC). These two authors seem modern to us now because they overtly challenge or ignore magical thinking, with its supernatural explanations for disaster. It is the absence or inadequacy of providential interpretation that draws history towards tragedy, as it does in Shakespeare's drama and the great panoramic 19th-century novels such as Tolstoy's *War and Peace* (1863–9).

Aristotle versus Plato

But tragedy, Aristotle famously affirms, is 'both more philosophical and more serious than history'. This is, he claims, because 'poetry speaks more of universals, history of particulars', or 'poetry tends to make general statements, while those of history are particular'. That is to say, history simply tells us what actually happened, but poetry aims at a higher and broader kind of truth. It represents what could or would happen, according to the criteria of probability or necessity. Historians will rightly object that this is an absurdly limited view of their subject. Aristotle seems to be thinking of chronicle writing at its most grindingly literal, the mere accumulation of daily fact. You could say it was a matter of artistry. He deplored the attempt of the *Cypria* and the *Little Iliad*, lost epics about the Trojan War, to get everything in from the first inklings to the last dregs. Unlike Homer, who knew that a good plot needs selection. Aristotle's own principles suggest there is no reason why, in the hands of a true 'poet', history should not be every bit as philosophical as tragedy. What he is pointing to is the demand we should make of any story that has durable claims on our attention, whatever its means of expression. We need from it an insight – we might even wish to add, a foresight – into the way we should expect things to happen. Aristotle is saying that tragedy teaches us something about the logic of cause and effect. It does this through plots that show us, to put it at its simplest, that if or when you do *this* or fail to do *that*, you can expect *these* to be the consequences. Tragedy is in this sense thoroughly realistic. It tells us the truth about the way things are going to be – probably, inevitably.

In this respect, as in others, Aristotle is defending tragedy against the charges made against it, and indeed all poetry, by Plato. Virtually all writings about tragedy before Hegel are conducted in the courtroom set up by Plato. He brings two main charges against tragedy. First, that it is supremely *un*realistic, the mere imitation of an imitation, twice removed from the realm of Ideas in which true reality is located. The phenomenal world is itself a shadow of the Ideas in this transcendent sphere, and the wretched poet's fictions are just the shadow of a shadow. Neo-Platonists like Sir Philip Sidney would try to rescue poetry by claiming for it direct access to the golden domain of transcendent reality, but that's another story. Plato's second accusation is that tragedy provokes in the spectator all sorts of dangerous passions. When we suffer misfortune in real life, we should restrain our grief and anger: 'nothing is gained for the future by indignation'. If the misfortune is still remediable, then we should do something about it. 'Medicine must drown threnodies' (that is, 'laments for the dead'), as one translator rather strikingly has it.

There is a strong and continuing tradition of hostility to tragedy from Plato onwards. This hostility comes from what we would call, in political terms, both the Right and the Left. The former worry that tragedy gets people too excited; the latter, that it doesn't excite them enough. To this we must add the feminist charge that tragedy is a predominantly masculine institution, composed by men for men. Some hostility is bound up with a broader antagonism to the theatre in general, a tradition very ably studied by Jonas Barish. From Aristotle there derives the traditional case for the defence. This seeks to rebut the charge that tragedy presents the world as dark, violent, and incomprehensible, and that it rouses in spectators analogous feelings. The prosecution argues that tragedy falsifies the truth, exciting thoughts, ideas, and passions that endanger the security of the state, established law, political power, and the sovereignty of reason. The response of Aristotle and his successors in the 16th and 17th centuries is that tragedy is morally, politically, psychologically, and theologically sound, a loyal and faithful servant to established power, in the state and in the individual. This is never entirely convincing.

Aristotle tries to meet Plato's second main objection about tragedy's effect on our passions through his famously enigmatic formula: 'through the arousal of pity and fear effecting the *katharsis* of such emotions'. A great deal of ink has been spilt on the question of what Aristotle meant by this, let alone of whether he is right. Where exactly is this *katharsis* supposed to take place? In the head, the soul, the spirit, or the guts? Should we translate it as 'purification' or 'purgation'? Is it, to adapt one recent critic, a matter of holy water or castor oil? And whatever it is, does it take place on stage, within the action of the play, or off stage, in the spectator or reader?

Whatever Aristotle intended by the concept, and whatever his readers have made of it, we can still ask whether his choice of metaphor is just. Perhaps Plato is right – that the emotions excited by tragedy are *not* safely or entirely discharged. But perhaps this is a good thing. Is Plato right that 'nothing is gained for the future by indignation'? Is Aristotle right to restrict the tragic emotions to pity and fear? Commentators have worried away at this miserly formula, as for example by describing pity as 'the impulse to approach' and terror as 'the impulse to retreat'. Is 'pity' a strong enough word for the 'visceral intensity' of the Greek *eleos* and *oiktos*? Perhaps 'compassionate grief' would be better. And what about anger? From the first word of Homer's *Iliad* onwards, tragedy brims with raging men and women, with Senecan *furor* and Shakespearean 'wrath'. Does nothing of this spill over to touch the audience? Is this what Plato is worried about – that tragedy might drive us *mad*?

Chapter 2
Once upon a time

The death of tragedy?

Let us look more closely at the idea that 'real' tragedy belongs to the past. Let's consider the argument put forward by the critic George Steiner in his important book *The Death of Tragedy* (1961) that the 17th century marks the 'great divide' in the history of tragedy. The rationalism of the 18th-century Enlightenment spelt its impossibility, and for all their attraction to myths, heroes, and extreme passions, the optimism of the Romantics doomed their attempts to revive it. This would make the last true tragedy Racine's *Athalie* (1691), and the last true tragedy in English Milton's *Samson Agonistes* (1671), both, as it happens, based upon Old Testament subjects. Milton, says Steiner, was 'the last major poet to assume the total relevance of classic and Christian mythology'.

From this point of view, there have been only two historical periods that have produced tragedy, the real thing. The first was in 5th-century BC Athens; the second in an early modern Europe that owed much of its cultural vitality to the rediscovery of classical antiquity. These eras of collective artistic activity produced the masterpieces by Aeschylus, Sophocles, and Euripides, by Marlowe and Shakespeare, Corneille and Racine, on which all subsequent ideas of tragedy have been based. Though it is a long way from the theatre of Dionysus in ancient Athens to the Globe on the banks of the Thames in late Elizabethan London, and from there to the palace of Versailles in Louis XIV's France, the word 'tragedy' might be meaningful enough to stretch from Aeschylus to Shakespeare, from Euripides to Racine. But no further.

This is for three reasons. For all their manifest differences, Aeschylus, Shakespeare, and Racine have in common the fact that for them the world was infused with divinity. It was impossible to escape a sense of the sacred, of radical danger, of dread. Secondly, the plays that staged these perilous relations between the human and the divine drew on well-known stories about what it means to be seized by forces beyond comprehension. Between myth, legend, and history, the boundaries were blurred. What mattered was simply that these stories were at once sufficiently distant and familiar to carry authority, the burden of traditional experience. There was room for magic and miracle, for the supernatural to burst or glide through the fabric of everyday life. Not that tragedy was directly concerned with the everyday. It dealt with exceptional figures in whose fate could be read the extreme possibilities of existence. Sophocles' chorus sing of Antigone going to the extreme of daring (*ep' eschaton thrasous*, 853); Shakespeare's Apemantus tells Timon of Athens: 'The middle of humanity thou never knewest, but the extremity of both ends' (IV. iii. 302–3).

Thirdly and relatedly, the language of these plays was not that of everyday prose but verse, often of the loftiest quality. This was the only medium sufficiently complex, sublime, and mysterious to express intimations of divinity and the dread it inspired. Greek choral lyrics are dense and intricate hymns that tax the understanding and resist translation. Leading figures rise into song alongside the chorus or other characters, as Orestes and Electra do round the tomb of their father in Aeschylus' *Libation Bearers*, and Sophocles' Antigone and Creon on their final appearances. Music and song do not play such a conspicuous role in Shakespeare or Racine, but passages and scenes require the lyric elevation of the voice, as for example with Juliet's 'Gallop apace, you fiery-footed steeds' (III. ii. 1), Othello's 'Farewell the tranquil mind, farewell content' (III. iii. 348), and Cleopatra's 'Give me my robe. Put on my crown. I have / Immortal longings in me' (V. ii. 275–6). The verse of French classical tragedy rejoices in its musicality. W. H. Auden remarks that you can no more hope to appreciate Racine's *Phèdre* without having heard a great performance than you can Wagner's *Tristan and Isolde*. The great 19th-century French actress Rachel, a legendary Phèdre, had the vocal range of an opera singer. As for the complexity of thought and feeling embodied in the most memorable monologues – by Hamlet and Macbeth, by the emperor Auguste in Corneille's *Cinna*, or Racine's Titus and Bérénice – for these only verse of the highest quality is adequate.

At first glance, the comparison with modern drama suggests only poverty: no gods, no collective myths, no great public figures, no poetry to speak of. The tragedy of the Greeks, of Shakespeare and Racine, was not a hard act to follow. It was impossible.

Do the gods look down?

This is a very elevated view of the past, and it points to a problem about generalization in which tragedy takes a particular interest. The loftier your viewpoint, the less difference you will see between particular items on the ground, such as people for instance. Charlie Chaplin averred that 'Life is a tragedy when seen in close-up, but a comedy in long-shot.' Do the gods, or God and his angels, look down on our doings in close-up or long-shot? Are they watching at all? At the moment of capitulation to his mother, Shakespeare's Coriolanus exclaims: 'The gods look down, and this unnatural scene / They laugh at' (V. iii. 185–6). In *Measure for Measure* Isabella thinks of the angels weeping at 'man, proud man' and the 'fantastic tricks' he plays before high heaven. If they had our human spleens, they 'would all themselves laugh mortal' (II. ii. 120–6). Convinced of her unforgivable guilt, Racine's Phèdre asks how she can endure the gaze of the sacred sun from whom she is descended, and how she will endure the sight of her father, judge of the underworld

(IV. vi. 1273–94). In Racine's universe, there's no place to hide. This leads Lucien Goldmann to generalize: 'Tragedy can be defined as a spectacle under the permanent observation of a deity.' But can we be sure? How do we know?

In Racine the goddess Vénus does not appear in person, as her counterpart Aphrodite does in the play by Euripides that he's re-writing, *Hippolytus*. So does her rival Artemis, near the end, though she absents herself from the scene of her disciple's dying. In Greek tragedy it is hard to know whether all the gods are watching all the time, or some of them some of the time, and how much, exactly, they care. In a magnificent vase painting (Figure 7) they seem blissfully unconcerned with the dramatic events beneath them, the horses driven crazy by a bull from the sea and a goading fury, the charioteer Hippolytus trying to control them, the helpless pitying human witness. Do the gods look down? Not here. Yet in Homer they do more than look down: they hurl themselves into the fray and fight with each other. Sheer folly, thinks Apollo, for the sake of mere mortals who flourish and wither like leaves on the tree (*Iliad*, 21. 461–7). How can you tell the difference between them? And yet the Homeric gods cannot help getting involved, for the sheer hell of it.

Tragedy is much concerned with the temptation and perhaps inevitability of generalizing in the face of this particular life and death, this mother, this son, this sister, this loved one, here and now, before our very eyes. So too with the urge to generalize about Tragedy in the face of *this* tragedy.

Here the rivalry between different versions of the same story is instructive. It is sometimes said that when the Athenian audiences sat down to watch tragedy at the festival of the City Dionysia, 'they all knew the story'. Well, yes and no. They would have been familiar with the general outlines of *what* has to happen, but who could be certain *how* it would happen this time? Agamemnon will die when he comes back from Troy, but who will kill him? In Aeschylus it is

7. Are the gods watching (over) us?

his wife Clytemnestra. But in a vase painting from around the time of the *Oresteia*, probably just before, it is her lover Aegisthus (Figure 8). Behind the shrinking dying king we see the impressive figure of Electra, the daughter who will help ensure retribution. Electra plays a critical role in the versions of her brother Orestes' revenge by all three tragedians, yet each time she is different. It's the same with the stories of Oedipus, his parents and children. We know that Euripides wrote an *Antigone* in which the heroine marries Haemon and they have a child called Maion – very different from Sophocles. Every time a story is told or a text is performed it will be different, and hence in some sense re-written. The legacy bequeathed by the Greek tragedians has itself been endlessly re-written, by Seneca in 1st-century AD Rome, by Racine in 17th-century France, by the composer Gluck in the later 18th century. The re-writing continues. Take the tale of Phaedra and Hippolytus, for example. This has been designed for performance by choreographers, composers, poets, and dramatists including Martha Graham (1962), Benjamin Britten (1975), Tony Harrison (*Phaedra Britannica*, 1975), and Brian Friel (*Living Quarters*, 1977).

8. **Death of Agamemnon**

As for the gods and religious belief: how much does it matter that the words 'Apollo', 'Zeus', 'the Furies', or indeed 'God', do not instantly strike fear into us, as they once did for others? Or that when Hamlet speaks of a 'divinity that shapes our ends' and the 'special providence in the fall of a sparrow' (V. ii. 10, 165–6), his faith commands less assent from listeners than it once did? Or that fewer spectators and readers are likely to believe in the religious conversions at the end of Corneille's *Polyeucte* (1641–2)? When Nietzsche announces that 'God is dead', does this mark an unbridgeable chasm between us now and them then?

But not everyone on the planet has heard Nietzsche's message, let alone assented to it. In any case, when we step into the domain of art, we suspend some of our everyday beliefs and risk being grasped by others. For the time being at least – who knows how long after? – Dionysus can enter our imagination. And even if we don't believe in Aphrodite and Dionysus, or God and the Devil, or ghosts for that matter, we can still recognize what they 'stand for'. (Or think that we do.) We can translate them into our own new myths, as Nietzsche did with Apollo and Dionysus, and Freud with Eros and Thanatos. We can read the ancient myths of divine punishment in modern terms, as Shelley and Marx did with Prometheus, as Freud did with the Oedipus legend, and Albert Camus with *The Myth of Sisyphus* (1942). These translations are of course interpretations.

But the divine always requires interpretation. Were the ancient Athenians sure what their gods 'stood for', and what the punishments suffered by their victims 'meant'? This was one of the main motives in Greek tragedy, to inquire into the mysterious and never ultimately knowable nature of divinity. The chorus in Aeschylus' *Agamemnon* pray to 'Zeus-whoever-you-are' (160). Zeus, Apollo, Aphrodite, Artemis, Dionysus: these are forces beyond human comprehension, ferocious and unpredictable. It is with this desire to make sense of them that the modern reader and spectator can identify, the attempt to translate into the light of day the obscure forces that govern us, our actions, and the course of the world. The names we give them are part of this doomed assault on the darkness.

Sacred and secular

The ways in which the Greek tragedians characterized the darkness are of course different from ours. In Sophocles' *Antigone*, the chorus sing of the 'wonders' that fill the earth (332), including – most wonderful of all – mankind. No single English word will do justice to the power of the Greek epithet *deinos* – wonderful, terrible, awesome, sacred. 'Dread' may come nearest to it. This is what Sophocles, Shakespeare, and Racine had in common. We hear it in the oaths and curses, in the appeals to 'heaven and hell' and 'ministers of grace', to fiends and devils, and demons and angels, and more obliquely when characters gesture, as Racine's Phèdre does, to *Vénus toute entière à sa proie attachée* ('Venus wholly fastened to her prey', I. iii. 306).

But were the audiences at the first performance of the *Bacchae*, *Hamlet*, and *Phèdre* unanimous in their religious beliefs? Of course not. We know from the way Aristophanes lampoons Euripides in several of his extant plays, most notably the *Frogs*, that the tragedian aroused powerful disagreements in his audience, not least because of his apparent disrespect for the gods. The conflict between traditional belief and modern scepticism is wrought into the very texture of Euripides' plays – as it is into Shakespeare's. Think of the discrepancy in *King Lear* between Gloucester's superstition and his bastard son Edmund's all too modern rationalism, or the rift between Othello's religious language and Iago's sophisticated cynicism.

Nevertheless, for all the conflicts within the worlds out of which these plays issued, we must acknowledge the great historical division between classical tragedy and *everything* afterwards. Whatever premonitions there had been in the pagan world, Christianity introduced to the West a nexus of new beliefs in the future, in re-birth and redemption and resurrection. The words inspired in Horatio by the dying Hamlet are inconceivable in Sophocles: 'flights of angels sing thee to thy rest' (V. ii. 313). Christianity changed the meaning of hope. Through its great central image of Christ on the cross, it also changed the meaning of suffering. Christian faith was bound to dilute the pagan vision of tragedy and the grimmer beliefs on which it depended, beliefs in fatality, in rampant and triumphant divinities, in temporal recurrence and a shadowy, joyless afterlife. No post-pagan artist in Europe could hope to escape from the idea of hope disseminated by Christianity, and bequeathed to the increasingly secular societies of the 19th century. Not at least until these hopes were challenged by new dreads, the fears that have come to plague the so-called secular societies of the West, the dark side of their godlessness and the threat of other religions. But the religion of others has (almost) always been a source of dread.

There is a famous dictum of I. A. Richards, that 'The least touch of any theology which has a compensating heaven to offer the tragic hero is fatal.' There is a good deal more to Christianity than the idea of a 'compensating heaven', and if Christianity provided new forms of hope, it also supplied new forms of despair. To these Marlowe's Dr Faustus gives memorable expression, as does Othello when he looks at the corpse of his wife: 'When we shall meet at count / This look of thine will hurl my soul from heaven, / And fiends will snatch at it' (V. ii. 280–2). We might think nothing could be *more* tragic than being hurled to hell from the brink of bliss. Behind the redeeming Son of God, there lurks the shadow of God the Father, who can easily be confused with the God of the Old Testament, just but no less ferociously swift to punish transgressors than his Greek counterparts. Consider the unfortunate Uzzah, who touches the sacred Ark of the Covenant when it seems to be falling and is instantly struck down (*2 Samuel*, 6, 6–7). Compare him with the Philoctetes who just puts a foot wrong by stepping in a holy place, and is marked for life by the wound he carries.

The demons and devils and witches and prophets have never been firmly expunged from the collective imagination, whether by Christianity or any other enlightening movement. The so-called Enlightenment of the 18th century did not banish the darkness for ever. And a wholly secular society, from which all sense of the sacred has been extirpated, is no more conceivable than a world without darkness, a life without night. What Sophocles, Shakespeare, and Racine share is the effort to stage the points of convergence at which the light and darkness meet, the sacred and secular, divine power and human reason. The ages that produced their drama were not characterized by stable coherent belief. It was precisely the conflicts to which they gave expression, between old religion and new politics, between traditional faith and modern rationalism, between the sacred and the secular.

Poetry

What of the charge that modern drama cannot match the elevation required of tragedy and displayed by its great antecedents? There is the interesting case of opera (or music-drama), and also of ballet (or dance-drama). The Florentine enthusiasts who began to develop in the 1590s what we have come to call opera saw it as the heir to Greek tragedy. Yet when Jacopo Peri's *Euridice* was first performed in 1601, the allegorical figure of Tragedy announced in the prologue: 'Behold, I change my gloomy buskins and dark robes to awaken in the heart sweeter emotions.' Is most opera simply too beautiful, too concerned with the 'sweeter emotions', to arouse the pain, the pity, and terror we expect from tragedy? Most perhaps – but not all. There are works and there are singers capable of expressing pain and grief amidst, or even despite, the beauty of the music. This is also true of the chamber form of lieder by Franz Schubert (1797–1828) and Hugo Wolf (1860–1903), for example. And where the fuller form of 'music-drama' is concerned, there's a case for seeing in the emotional, intellectual, and symbolic force of certain 19th- and 20th-century operas the true legacy of the tragic dramas of the

Greeks and Shakespeare, in Wagner's *Tristan and Isolde* (1859) and *Ring* cycle (1869–76), in Béla Bartók's *Bluebeard's Castle* (1911) and Alban Berg's *Wozzeck* (1923), or more recently in the American composer John Adams's *The Death of Klinghoffer* (1991). This last – based on the hijacking of the cruise-ship the *Achille Lauro* in 1985 by Palestinian terrorists – has certainly addressed and stirred the kind of controversy that is tragedy's territory. Nor should we ignore the case of dance in its association with music, especially when it stages an expressly tragic narrative, as the choreographer Martha Graham did with Medea's story (1946) and Phaedra's (1962).

Even leaving music and dance aside, there is more to be said about the resources of modern theatre. In the early years of the 19th century, Hegel argued that drama should be regarded as the supreme art because human speech is the only medium fully adequate to the presentation of spiritual life, and *dramatic* speech unites the objectivity of epic and the subjectivity of lyric. Drama requires the physical components of performance – the bodies of the actors, the arts of stage design, lighting, and sound – but all these merely provide the material basis 'out of which the language of poetry is in its free domination asserted as the commanding central focus upon and around which all else really revolves'. This is exactly what gets challenged in modern drama: the adequacy of speech, the dominating centrality of poetry.

In a narrow sense of the term, 'poetry' plays a significant role in verse plays by Yeats, Eliot, and Paul Claudel (whose *Le Soulier de satin* has been hailed by Steiner as 'one of the few plays in modern literature that comes near to being great tragedy'). Also in arresting new versions of ancient Greek classics by Ezra Pound, Wole Soyinka, Tony Harrison, Seamus Heaney, and others. Irish writers have taken a notably strong interest in the Greeks. There have been some great dramatists who have also written poetry outside the theatre, including Ibsen, Lorca, Brecht, and Beckett. But if we allow a distinction between 'verse' and 'poetry' in a larger sense of the term, we may wish to recognize a difference between poetry 'in' the theatre and poetry 'of' the theatre.

Ibsen is often taken as a point of departure for modern drama, and rightly so. Of the 26 plays that he wrote, he is now best known for the last 12, all written in prose, beginning with *The Pillars of Society* (1877) and concluding with *When We Dead Awaken* (1899). (There is a case for reading them as a concerted sequence.) Of the 14 preceding plays, almost all were written in verse on subjects from history, epic, legend, and folklore. They include, most importantly, two plays not originally designed for performance: *Brand* (1866) and *Peer Gynt* (1867). But in 1874 Ibsen wrote famously to Edmund Gosse defending his decision to write one of them in prose, the gigantic *Emperor and Galilean*:

> My new play is no tragedy in the old style; what I wanted to portray was people, and it was precisely for that reason that I did not allow them to speak with 'the tongues of angels'.

The critical break in Ibsen's work is the deliberate choice of restriction, forfeiture, sacrifice. The descent is tantamount to a fall – from the plenitude of poetry to the penury of prose. Yet 'poetry', in the fullest sense of the term, is not entirely banished. On the contrary, it is, as Freud would describe it – and he recognized a colleague in Ibsen – 'repressed'. Poetry returns to take its revenge in those symptoms of neurotic disturbance and desire that we vaguely call Ibsen's 'symbols': wild ducks, white horses, towers, strangers from the sea, rat-wives and their dogs. E. M. Forster described the Norwegian writer as a Romantic guerrilla waging a rearguard action against the world of bourgeois prose into which he had had the misfortune to survive. From this subversive perspective, prose is not the norm from which poetry deviates; poetry is the norm from which prose represents a catastrophic lapse.

Succeeding dramatists have found other ways, often more versatile, to stage the frustrations of desire: Bertolt Brecht and Federico

García Lorca, for example, both of whom struggled against vicious political repression in the 1930s, in Germany and Spain respectively. Yet the play Lorca completed just a few months before he was murdered by the Fascists in August 1936 comes close to Ibsen in its formal repression. Reading *The House of Bernarda Alba* to friends, Lorca is supposed to have exclaimed with triumph after each scene: 'Not a drop of poetry! . . . Pure realism!' This is nonsense; the poet was teasing. There is no literal escape for the women trapped in this House of Death, and no soaring transcendence through language. Yet poetry persists in their desire for a better life and another world. This is vividly embodied in the defiance not only of the youngest daughter but less predictably of her grandmother. The monstrous matriarch Bernarda Alba tries to keep this 80-year-old woman locked up, but María Josefa keeps getting out. She wants to marry a beautiful man from the shore of the sea. In the last act she comes on carrying a lamb in her arms, singing to her baby. No poetry indeed.

Chapter 3
The living dead

Ghosts

Tragedy is full of them. In the first surviving complete tragedy that
has come down to us, Aeschylus' *Persians* (472 BC), the ghost of
the dead King Darius rises from his tomb. He pronounces
judgement on his overweening son, Xerxes, who has squandered
the wealth of the mightiest empire the world has ever known.
King, father, god (for he has been deified in the underworld),
Darius speaks from beyond the grave with an authority we rarely
find in subsequent tragedies. Even the immortal gods whose
authority is beyond question are often hard to understand,
speaking as they do through oracles and prophets and seers, like
Cassandra and Teiresias.

In the central play of the Oresteian trilogy, Agamemnon's son and
daughter converge on his tomb, along with the chorus, to lament his
passing and seek inspiration for the justice his spirit demands. But
Agamemnon does not rise from the underworld – unlike some other
murdered kings and fathers. The ghost of Hamlet's father does walk
abroad, but where does he come from? The purgatory that good
Protestants are no longer supposed to believe in? Does he bring 'airs
from heaven or blasts from hell' (I. iv. 22)? Why does his son feel
'Prompted to my revenge by heaven *and* hell' (II. ii. 586, emphasis
added)? We may note that the roots of our English word 'ghost'

seem linked, in the dark, backward abysm of time, with fury and anger.

Ghosts in tragedy are invariably associated with judgement and retributive justice: in Shakespeare's *Richard III* and *Macbeth*, for example. Yet a story that simply vindicates the dead and approves the justice they seek is not going to be tragic. A cautionary tale perhaps, but one that will only turn into tragedy when justice presents a problem, a quandary, not least for the person to whom the ghostly spirit appears. Hamlet gets to see the ghost of his father and Orestes does not, but both have to act *for* the dead – who are not yet fully dead, but living on in the hearts and minds of their sons.

A ghost is unnerving (at least) because it seems alive, like the person we once knew. It has come back from the bourn from which no traveller is supposed to. It has crossed a boundary that should be impassable. It's almost as bad as incest. A ghost is confusing because it throws into doubt the difference between the living and the dead. It can make the living feel dead or look dead. When Lady Macbeth tries in vain to wash the blood from her hands, she's already a ghost and we're watching a soul in hell. The Greek word for the 'ghost' of Darius is *eidōlon*, meaning a phantom or any unsubstantial form (we eventually get our word 'idol' from it). Agamemnon uses it to deplore the treachery of appearances (*Agamemnon*, 839). He would agree with Duncan that there's no art to find the mind's construction in the face (*Macbeth*, I. iv. 11–12). Sophocles' Odysseus also uses the word *eidōlon* when the sight of his enemy Ajax's humiliation at the hands of the goddess Athene makes him think how fragile we are, friend and foe alike (*Ajax*, 126). This is what the gods can do to us. Compared with them, we're no more than shadows and shows without substance. This is the conclusion Macbeth reaches when he reflects on the living death to which he has reduced himself and the world around him:

> Life's but a walking shadow, a poor player
> That struts and frets his hour upon the stage,

And then is heard no more. It is a tale
Told by an idiot, full of sound and fury,
Signifying nothing.

(V. v. 23–7)

In tragedy the supernatural does not always materialize. Gods and
ghosts do not always speak, nor do they and their ministering
angels always appear – one hesitates to say – in the flesh. There are
ghosts in *Hamlet* and *Macbeth* but not in *Othello* and *King Lear*.
These latter two plays are less directly concerned than the former
with the past, with memory, mourning, and revenge. Yet in a broad
sense, tragedy always deals with toxic matter bequeathed by the
past to the present. In personal terms, this often means what
fathers and mothers have passed on to their children in the form of
duties, loyalties, passions, and injuries. When these conflict with
each other, as they do for Orestes, Electra, and Hamlet, it may take
violence to resolve them – or more time than a play can normally
represent. The *Oresteia* is a striking example of what can be
achieved through a sequence of plays. So too is Richard Wagner's
cycle of four music dramas, *The Ring of the Nibelung* (produced
1869–76), which owes a great deal to Aeschylus. Novels are
another matter. But within the confines of the single play there
may not be time to lay the living dead to rest. As Berowne (or
Biron) says, 'That's too long for a play' (*Love's Labour's Lost*,
V. ii. 865).

The ghosts so far considered bear down on the nearest and dearest
who have killed them, or those who must mourn them and avenge
them. But there is a more political aspect to the living dead. They
also bear heavily on a whole city, people, community, or culture, in
so far as they embody values, ideas, and ethics that challenge the
present and obstruct the future. The living dead are by nature
conservative, if not reactionary. Like Lorca's Bernarda Alba, they
insist that the world remain as it was for them. Who needs tragedy?
One answer is that it's a way of honouring and allaying ghosts
collective as well as personal. This is a way of understanding tragedy

as socially no less than psychologically progressive, a means of freeing the future from the past.

From this point of view, tragedy stages moments of crisis in a community's understanding of itself, moments when it risks being torn apart by conflicting beliefs about the gods, political authority, relations between the generations and the sexes, between natives and immigrants. These beliefs invariably have a temporal aspect to them. 'Thou metst with things dying, I with things new-born', says the Shepherd to the Clown in *The Winter's Tale* (III. iii. 110–11), at the point when the play turns from tragedy towards penance, reparation, healing and re-birth, from winter to spring. But what of the dying things that live malignantly on, blocking the way to the future? Thomas Hardy voices the caution instilled by tragedy when he writes 'if way to the Better there be, it exacts a full look at the Worst'. *If.* Tragedies try to imagine the worst, while acknowledging with Edgar of *King Lear* that: 'The worst is not / So long as we can say "This is the worst"' (IV. i. 27–8).

In the *Oresteia* it becomes clear that there is no *logical* escape from the nightmare of eternal recurrence on which the principle of retributive justice depends. An eye for an eye till the end of time. The logic of revenge is at once impeccable and intolerable. To those wholly caught up in its structure, the duty of retaliation is self-evident, the guilt of the victim is patent, the justification of the avengers – even if they must sacrifice their own lives – absolute. This is not tragic for *them*. They can exult in death, both their own and others. But to those outside its structure, or anyone less than wholly absorbed in it, the logic of revenge is a nightmare whose only issue is death and more death. Is there not some other way forward, that would break free of the past, leaving it dead and truly buried?

These are questions posed by Ariel Dorfman's remarkably successful play, *Death and the Maiden*, inspired by the Chilean commission appointed in 1990 to investigate the human rights violations of the Pinochet years. The dramatist speaks of wishing 'to write a contemporary tragedy in an almost Aristotelian sense, a work of art that might help a collective to purge itself, through pity and terror'. Aeschylus would have recognized his desire to strengthen 'a fragile democracy . . . by expressing for all to see the deep dramas and sorrows and hopes that underlie its existence'.

Heroes

The past is not always so obviously baneful. It can provide models of conduct that look positively heroic by comparison with the degraded contemporary world. For the Greeks, 'the heroes' belonged to a privileged time in the past when gods and human beings mixed more freely than now. A hero such as Heracles or Theseus or Achilles was the product of a sexual union between god and mortal, half-human, half-divine. The great warriors who fought at Troy belonged to 'the heroic age'. They embodied values which were thought of as heroic, and largely still are: courage, pride, a high sense of honour, especially their own. But heroes are more at home in epic than in tragedy, where they are exposed to more complex ordeals and harder questions are asked of them. Can war make peace, or does it just propagate more war, like revenge? What happens when the soldiers come home? Do their family, city, and country welcome their bloodstained bodies and minds with open arms? Agamemnon and Coriolanus provide two signal cases when the warrior's triumphant return goes wrong. As his rival Aufidius puts it, Coriolanus cannot move from 'th' casque to th' cushion' (IV. vii. 43) – that is, from the battlefield to the council-chamber.

Do heroes belong in the modern world? Or are they a liability, an anachronism, even an embarrassment? In the hands of the Greeks and Shakespeare, these questions are complex and the answers are various. The leading figures in Sophocles have some things in common. Ajax, Heracles, Antigone, Oedipus, Electra, Philoctetes: they cleave to a high idea of themselves. They are passionate, purposive, resolute, rigorous, indomitable, difficult. They command *admiration*, in an old sense of the term that connotes wonder but not necessarily approval, moral or otherwise. Or to use an associated word familiar to Shakespeare and his contemporaries, they provide 'mirrors' for us to contemplate. They are exemplary, but they are not necessarily examples to follow. They are glamorous, charismatic, spectacular. But in tragedy they become a problem, not least for those around them, wives like Tecmessa in *Ajax*, sisters like Ismene in *Antigone*, rulers like Theseus in *Oedipus at Colonus*. From an everyday perspective, the hero seems like a reckless extremist, even when she has right on her side, as Antigone does. In Euripides the heroic is always wrong, a baneful hangover from bygone times. This is especially true of the plays that re-stage some of Homer's heroic material to expose the murderous realities of war – *Hecuba* and *Trojan Women*.

As for Shakespeare, there are certainly men who embody the conventionally heroic virtues – men such as Hotspur and Hamlet's father, Mark Antony and Caius Martius. Othello and Macbeth also, great warriors and generals fêted by their rulers and employers – and needed by them. But in every case they are placed in positions that expose their dangerous and sometimes murderous anachronism. They are all contrasted with a more modern figure, cooler, more cautious, more stealthy, like the Prince Hal who will become King Henry V or the Octavius Caesar who will become the Emperor Augustus, 'the universal landlord'. Not that the right young man always inherits the future. It is not young Hamlet who claims the throne of Denmark but young Fortinbras, who is more of a chip off the old block.

Hell on earth

Modern tragedy has found new forms for the living dead. We see fewer ghosts, for all the play our fiction and films now make with them. But they are there, or here, still waiting to haunt us. Freud has given us one new way of thinking about our ghosts as 'the return of the repressed'. We can translate the Aeschylean Furies into these terms, especially when we hear Athene warning her citizens that they must not repudiate *to deinon*, 'dread' (*Eumenides*, 698), but find some way to acknowledge, honour, and even embrace it. From Ibsen onwards artists have kept repeating this warning. More than one of his plays could have been entitled *Ghosts*; so too could Arthur Miller's guilt-ridden *After the Fall* (1964). The fiercely confined settings of Ibsen's drama spawn new kinds of ghost, not only those of the past but also of a future that will not come to birth, like the child in Hedda Gabler's womb. Hence the extraordinary force of the unborn child who haunts the marriage of George and Martha in Edward Albee's *Who's Afraid of Virginia Woolf?* (1962).

The idea of a 'living death' looks like a modern complement to the old belief in ghosts, the haunters, the revenants, the undead. It's a vision of death-in-life, a life so drained of meaning, value, purpose, and joy that it seems like death, being dead before you are dead. It's a version of hell on earth, more inert, more soundproof, more blank than others. In the modern era it tends to be focused in images of imprisonment, silence, and madness. From the Fall of the Bastille onwards, the dread of being unjustly incarcerated, entombed, and forgotten invades the modern imagination. Also the dream of being released, as in Beethoven's opera *Fidelio* (1814). Think of all the prisons that modern artists explore and expose to view, the prisons that drive people mad and that madness creates. At the climax of Eugene O'Neill's masterpiece, *A Long Day's Journey into Night* (1956), Mary Tyrone makes her terrible final entrance, the beloved wife and mother now lost to drugs, beyond hope. 'The Mad Scene. Enter Ophelia!' cracks her elder son Jamie. The mad Ophelia is one good model for the many modern figures who lose all touch with the world and turn into the living dead.

Yet we can find visions of this nightmare back amongst the ancient Greeks. Sophocles' late play *Philoctetes* (409 BC) is about the archer who was bitten by a snake on the way to Troy and abandoned by his colleagues on the island of Lemnos. They discover that if they are to conquer Troy they need him and the sacred invincible bow he has inherited from Heracles, so they come back to fetch him, or it, or both. He is not keen to help them. The desert island is one of the great creations of Greek tragedy. It is a wilderness untouched by humanity, where 'Man's life is cheap as beast's', as Lear puts it (II. iv. 267). Only the gift of the bow enables its wounded wielder to eat and save himself from being eaten. His only companions are the wound and the bow, and he lives with the horror of dying alone. Philoctetes' play is about the possibility of healing but also about its difficulty, and even perhaps its desirability. 'You do me wrong to take me out o'th'grave', Lear murmurs in rebuke to those around him (IV. vi. 38), as he emerges from the madness in which he has been lost. Other figures in Greek tragedy might echo the sentiment, such as Euripides' Heracles (in the play named after him) and Agave (in *Bacchae*). Both return from the crazed state inflicted on them by the gods to discover the corpses of the loved ones they have murdered in their absence from themselves.

Oliver Sacks tells an exemplary tale about living death. In *Awakenings* (1973), he describes some of the victims of the sleeping-sickness pandemic after the Great War. (Harold Pinter's fine play *A Kind of Alaska* (1982) draws directly on Sacks's book.) Fifty years later, under the influence of the drug L-Dopa, Sacks's patients were forcibly woken from their frozen limbo. The effects were frequently violent and always unpredictable. Like Greek gods, you might say. Sacks tells us of the gnawing and biting compulsions released in one of his sleepers, 'Frances D.', the savage appetites and passions. These seemed to be at once alien and not alien to her 'real self'. The patient herself felt them to be:

> in some sense releases or exposures or disclosures or confessions of very deep and ancient parts of herself, monstrous creatures from her unconscious and from unimaginable physiological depths below the unconscious, pre-historic and perhaps pre-human landscapes whose features were at once utterly strange to her, yet mysteriously familiar, in the manner of certain dreams.

So there are still more things in heaven and earth, and the

illimitable depths underneath and behind us, than are dreamt of in our daily philosophies.

Living with the dead

How should the living remember the dead? Memory is sometimes thought of as a kind of space, a chamber or treasure-house or even a theatre. But it is also an action and process. And tragedies are much concerned with memory in action, *as* action, specifically the action of mourning. The origins of tragedy may be bound up with mourning rites for a dead hero or king. We can readily imagine that as such rites became more elaborate, they entailed more than praise of the dead man, the telling of tales about him and the re-enactment of his feats. They would also have started to ask questions about how he died and why. This process requires witnesses who may themselves have been key players and agents in the dead man's life and death. A tragedy is amongst other things a kind of inquest, and its enquiries can extend to the rites of mourning themselves.

Tragedies like to represent such rites going wrong. Think of the perverted mourning rites round Agamemnon's tomb in Aeschylus' *Libation Bearers*, or of Antigone's frantically improvised burial of her brother Polyneices' corpse in Sophocles' play, or of the disgraceful scenes round Ophelia's tomb in *Hamlet*, or the chaos around Hedvig's corpse in Ibsen's *The Wild Duck*. We see a corresponding desire to get things right, to see the dead figures properly laid to rest, especially if they have been figures of controversy in life, like Ajax and Heracles and Oedipus. Think too of the anxious desire to honour the dead at the end of Shakespeare's *Romeo and Juliet* and *Julius Caesar*.

All these examples involve mourning as a collective activity: public commemoration rather than private memory. One of the distinctive features of modern tragedy is that it takes such an interest in private, even secret, mourning. One of Wordsworth's 'Lucy poems' is exemplary in this respect, 'She dwelt among the untrodden ways'.

In the eyes of the world Lucy was a non-entity: 'But she is in her grave, and oh, / The difference to me!' Yet the writing of this poem, its publication, and continued reading begin to make Lucy a public person. This is a paradox embodied in many modern texts and works of art that seek to share griefs, bereavements, and traumas that would otherwise remain private, neglected, unnoticed.

In this respect, tragedy spills out beyond the confines of drama, and even of fiction, into historical writing, documentary journalism, and photography. The tragedy here may be in the fact that the suffering *has been* forgotten and the act of reparation has come too late. The final chorus in Brecht's play *The Life of Galileo* speaks of the future that lies ahead for his scientific work: 'But we hope you'll keep in mind / He and I were left behind.' Brecht thought Hiroshima changed our understanding of that future. In a postscript to the American production of the play in 1947, he wrote: 'The day the bomb was dropped will not easily be forgotten by anyone who spent it in the United States.' But until recently few could forget because few had known of the 750 American servicemen who died in April 1944 when they were ambushed by German torpedo boats off the coast of Devon during a training exercise for D-Day. On the instructions of General Eisenhower this remained largely a secret for nearly 40 years. Similarly with the death of the 5,000 men on the British troop ship *Lancastria* sunk at the mouth of the Loire in June 1940, the biggest maritime disaster in British history, and the 8,000 German civilians aboard the *Wilhelm Gustloff* sunk by a Russian submarine in January 1945, the biggest maritime disaster of all time. All these were tragedies suppressed at the time by the authorities (the *Guardian*, 24 April 2004). Brecht would not have been surprised.

In the Western world, we do not live as close to the dead as our ancestors did in the Middle Ages and as other peoples still do, cheek by jowl with their graves and physical remains. But we still suffer from primitive dread about the dead-but-not-gone. This seems to be connected at a deep instinctual level to our sense of justice, the justice we owe to them and they to us. We still feel horror at the desecration of a corpse, whether it is abandoned and exposed to the elements, like Polyneices', or it rots unmarked in a mass grave. We still hear in our heads the voices of authority, the figures to whom we once looked up and perhaps still do, for judgement.

Modern psychology has provided us with new ways of understanding these terrors and traumas. Other more material sciences have helped us recognize how profoundly the physical world is composed by the past. Archaeology, environmental sciences, biological anthropology, genetics: these have shown how our landscapes, our dwellings, our cities, our bodies are built up from the past. How little we can do about so much we have inherited. Yet is there not always *some* choice in how we respond? We can destroy this ancient city and we can restore it again – and destroy another one. The fact that we know so much more about the genetic codes we carry inside us, about the foods and liquids we ingest, about the very air we inhale, this knowledge presents us with new dilemmas, new choices. We can never entirely free ourselves from the living dead, but we can strive to do justice – not only to them but also to ourselves, as we will in our turn become the living dead for future generations.

Yet some have much more choice than others. Is it always true, as Arthur Miller bravely contends, 'that we are made and yet are more than what made us'? Tragedy makes us wonder not only 'what made us' but also who 'we' are.

Chapter 4
Who's to blame?

'It is the cause'

Until quite a late stage Dickens was going to call one of his novels *Nobody's Fault*. It ended up as *Little Dorrit* (1855–7), but the acerbic phrase remains the heading of a key chapter. The filth of the slums that fostered contagious disease in the earlier *Bleak House* (1851–3) – the state of the sewers and graveyards and garbage amidst which poor Jo, the crossing-sweeper, ekes out his poisoned existence – these were not natural. Dickens was deriding a standard response to catastrophe, especially by the powers that be, that no one could possibly have foreseen or prevented it. It's an Act of God, or the gods, or a freak of nature, like an earthquake, a volcanic eruption, a meteor from outer space. Or as a leading American politician has phlegmatically put it: 'Stuff happens.' (But earthquakes *do* happen.) The other regular reaction is that someone *else* is to blame. Aliens, terrorists, immigrants, communists, Catholics, Jews, Muslims, women: the list of possible culprits is endless, as long as 'they' are monstrously different from 'us' – where they come from, what they believe, or what they look like.

Contagious disease does not select its victims with care. Terrorists choose their 'targets', but their bombs make no fine distinctions between those who happen to be in the wrong place at the wrong time – so-called civilians. War, famine, and plague: the traditional weapons of mass destruction are not much concerned with the responsibility of their victims for the conditions which launched them in the first place. Dickens insisted that the lethal state of the London underworld was everyone's business if not everyone's fault. No matter how innocent of its creation, no one in the vicinity was immune from its consequences. And where does the vicinity end? The kind of disaster in which tragedy takes a particular interest touches – and may engulf – all of us. Where does responsibility begin and end for the victims of a war, a famine, a plague, a tsunami?

Tragedy presents situations in which there is a desperate urgency to assign blame. This is the condition of Thebes at the start of Sophocles' *Oedipus Tyrannus*. It supplies the motive for the play's official action. Who is to blame for the plague that afflicts the whole city, the unborn children dying in their mothers' wombs? Sometimes there is no mystery at all. In *Bacchae*, for instance, where it's clear from the start that the Thebans, led by their young king Pentheus, have grossly offended the god Dionysus. They are asking for trouble and they duly get it. Yet at the end it's hard not to sympathize with the bereaved grandfather Cadmus when he passes judgement on the god for the monstrosity of his justice. Tragedies complicate the question of blame because they don't isolate the crime, the trial, and the judgement from living histories that continue to unfold around and through them. Even when we see for ourselves the act that unleashes collective disaster – when Shakespeare's conspirators murder Julius Caesar on stage, for example – this involves more than the guilt of a single figure for a single crime.

So who is to blame for a tragedy? One explanation is that it is a particular individual sometimes known as 'the tragic hero' or 'protagonist' (the latter comes from the Greek meaning 'first actor', as opposed to the second and third actors, who between them took all the roles). Another is that it is the gods or God, or some force or agency that can be credited with irresistible power to determine our lives, such as Fate, Fortune, the stars, history, or heredity. Thus Romeo, 'Then I defy you, stars' (V. i. 24). Or, most helplessly, Othello on the brink of murdering Desdemona: 'It is the cause, it is the cause, my soul' (V. ii. 1). But what is '*it*'?

Fatal error

Aristotle provided an influential answer when he called it *hamartia*. But what does it mean and how should we translate it? *Hamartia* is still sometimes thought of as a 'fatal flaw', as if it were simply an attribute of character. But it is important that Aristotle is talking about the possible types of tragic plot (*mythos*), which he insists is 'the first principle, and, so to speak, the soul of tragedy'. Tragedy is concerned with what people *do* rather than with who they *are*, he says. Success and failure, happiness and misery, good fortune and bad: this is what tragedies show us, not whether the people who enjoy and endure them are 'good' or 'bad'. Tragedy does not simply support our ideas of 'poetic justice'.

Nevertheless, Aristotle is not unconcerned with the ethical qualities of the characters in tragedy. The best kind of plot is one that most effectively excites the emotions of pity and fear, he says, and this will not be best achieved by showing the fall of a good man or the rise of a bad man, or indeed the fall of a bad man. There remains, Aristotle concludes,

> the figure who falls between these types. Such a man is one who is not preeminent in virtue and justice, and one who falls into affliction not because of evil and wickedness, but because of a certain fallibility (*hamartia*).

Others translate *hamartia* more simply as 'fault', 'mistake', or 'error'. And however much of a character's *propensity* to error we read into the concept, the primary emphasis seems to be on the error itself, the fault committed. To take a mild example, it's like a tennis serve that falls the wrong side of the line ('Fault!'). To take a graver example, Philoctetes wanders off the beaten path and into a sacred shrine guarded by a snake, who punishes his 'error'. Oedipus puts more than a foot wrong when he breaks two great taboos, killing his father and marrying his mother. So too does Orestes when he kills his mother; Medea and Heracles and Agave when they kill their own children; and Creon in *Antigone* when he refuses burial to Polyneices' body.

If we allow some latitude to the concept of error, the idea of making a mistake that has fatal consequences could be applied to Romeo's intervention between Mercutio and Tybalt, King Lear's division of the kingdom, and Macbeth's killing of Duncan. These are acts undertaken with very different degrees of volition, understanding, and consciousness, but they all take place in the play's present. By contrast, there are many plays in which the error occurs before the play begins. These include Claudius's murder of Hamlet's father; Oedipus' killing of Laius and marriage to Jocasta; and Joe Keller's suppression of the truth about the fatally flawed aircraft cylinders that doom 'all my sons' in Arthur Miller's play of that name (1947). The notion of error begins to lose force when it becomes more of a link in a chain, like the errors of the House of Atreus that stretch into the fathomless past, or when error has turned into an all-encompassing state, like the 'ancient grudge' from which the Montagues and Capulets seem unable (or unwilling) to escape, or the aftermath of war in which Euripides' Trojan Women are stranded, or any number of characters in modern drama from Büchner's Woyzeck (in the play named after him) to Beckett's Hamm and Clov in *Endgame*.

Aristotle makes the further recommendation that the character should make his or her fatal mistake in a state of ignorance. If Oedipus knew what he was doing at the time, we would be horrified. Sophocles' Deianeira does not know what she's doing (in *Women of Trachis*), nor do Euripides' Heracles and Agave, who are temporarily possessed, driven out of their wits. But what of Orestes? He knows exactly what he is doing but he's not always sure that he's right to be doing it. Orestes hopes and prays that he is a minister of justice, but whose justice? Hamlet is in a similar quandary. Othello knows what he is doing when he kills Desdemona but he imagines that he is a minister of justice rather than a murderer. King Lear does in one sense know what he's doing when he divides the kingdom, but he has no idea of its implications.

Then there's Medea and the Macbeths. Aristotle specifically deplores the case of the former, who knows what she is doing when she kills her children, as Heracles and Agave do not. What would he have made of Macbeth, who knows in advance he has no good reason to kill his kinsman, king, and guest? We may need to extend the idea of 'ignorance' to cover the great range of states in which terrible acts are committed. This would include the Macbeths' ignorance – and King Lear's – of the *consequences* of their acts. It might be better to turn the issue round and say that tragedies ask what it means to say that 'we know what we are doing'. Or indeed, that we know who 'we' are who are doing it (or in Hamlet's case, not doing it). Teiresias tells Oedipus: 'you are blind in your ears, in your mind, and in your eyes' (*Oedipus Tyrannus*, 371). '[H]e hath ever but slenderly known himself', one of Lear's daughters (Regan) says of him (I. i. 292–3). But this is generally true of characters in tragedy. They demonstrate the partiality with which we know ourselves. We cannot possibly know all the meanings of what we do, including all their consequences, unless like Teiresias we are cursed with the vision of the gods. As Arthur Miller painstakingly puts it, apropos of *All My Sons*: 'what I was after was the wonder in the fact that consequences of actions are as real as the actions themselves . . .'.

Aristotle's conception of *hamartia* is distinctly limited. It doesn't begin to address the intensity and complexity of guilt, the punitive judgements we endure in ourselves and pass on others. We suffer these judgements for things we did unwittingly, for things we should have done but didn't, for things that somebody else did – our parents, children, colleagues, fellows, anyone from whom we fail to dissociate ourselves, whether in our own eyes or others'. Such guilt is far more indiscriminately contagious than the notion of *hamartia* allows. It is closer to the sense of unavoidable *miasma*, pollution, or stain – 'the human stain', to borrow the title of a novel by Philip Roth (2000).

In league with the gods

There is not much blood, horror, or pollution in the rational world of Aristotle's *Poetics*. Nor is there any reference to the gods. They certainly provide another explanation for disaster. The *hamartia* committed by a human being seems trivial by comparison with the decision of a god or goddess to make something happen. As when, for example, at the start of Euripides' *Hippolytus*, Aphrodite announces that she is going to use Phaedra to destroy the eponymous hero. The young man has committed an error in devoting himself to another goddess, Artemis, thereby offending the goddess of sexual passion. The world of Greek tragedy is so riddled with gods that it is hard to stay on good terms with them all, not to put a foot wrong, especially when they are so sensitive to offence, so swift and fierce to punish. In Euripides the punishment can be out of all proportion to the offence, at least to human eyes, as it is in *Bacchae*. Translated into human terms, these divinities embody arbitrary power at its most frightening: the whim of the tyrant or the thug's knee-jerk retaliation to 'disrespect'.

But what has Phaedra done wrong? The 'error' she commits in falling for Hippolytus is caused by Aphrodite. Was it Aphrodite who made her mother mate with a bull to produce the Minotaur? You could call this a mistake, but if so, it's a mistake that has got so deep into the bloodstream that the vocabulary of choice, agency, and will begins to seem scarcely relevant. Phaedra derives her being from Crete, that dark, violent, primitive place with which so much that antedates the Olympian deities is associated. Behind, beneath, beyond the clear bright outlines of the sky-gods the Greeks acknowledged a prior realm of darkness that harboured forces much harder to name, including the children of night, the Furies.

Greek tragedies do not just expound beliefs about the gods; they debate them. And the most important aspects of this debate concern the points at which human beings and gods act *together*. This is the image used by Darius and his queen in *Persians*, when they try to explain how their son has committed his terrible *hamartia*: a god or a *daimōn* must have 'joined in' with him (724, 742). It takes two to make the tragic act happen, both the human agent and the divine or non-human. This is a helpful clue to the treatment of blame in tragedy, that there is never a singular cause. Indeed, two agencies represent the absolute minimum; there may turn out to be far more, a whole complex chain or sequence of causation.

Extremists

There is a further deficiency in Aristotle's formulations. It is misleading to think of the tragic character from a moral point of view as middling or intermediate, neither wholly virtuous nor vicious. 'Middling' is not the word we would use to describe the main characters in Greek tragedy. It makes them sound far too normal; indeed, they are often contrasted with other characters close by who *are* more normal, like Ismene in *Antigone*, Creon in *Oedipus Tyrannus*, or Chrysothemis in *Electra*. Horatio is asked to play a similar role as Mr Normal (at least in Hamlet's eyes). Passionate, reckless, daring, excessive, exceptional: those are the words more readily prompted by Clytemnestra and Antigone and Medea, Prometheus and Heracles and Oedipus. The same goes for the passionate extremism of Marlowe's Tamburlaine and Dr Faustus, Shakespeare's Romeo and Juliet, Othello, Macbeth, Coriolanus. And again for the extremists of French neoclassical drama, for Corneille's Horace, Camille, and Polyeucte, for Racine's Néron, Phèdre, and Athalie. Corneille convincingly proposes that virtue and vice are largely beside the point. A character is good for drama when it is vivid, brilliant, and intense.

Perhaps we should forget about morality, and think about myth, fantasy, appetite, and desire – everything we can safely enjoy on stage, in fiction, on screen; everything that has to be excluded or at least tempered in the rational everyday lives we try to lead 'outside'. We could add to this Freud's argument that what appeals to us about great characters on stage is precisely their enormity. All the sex and violence they commit – all their 'errors' – act out for us the desires and fears we have to repress. Of course tragic characters are primitive, barbaric, monstrous. They represent all that we have had to overcome in the cause of culture and civilization. As Nietzsche sardonically remarks:

> What an enormous price man had to pay for reason, seriousness, control over his emotions – those grand prerogatives and cultural showpieces! How much blood and horror lies behind all 'good things'!

So tragedy shows us what we are missing.

Finding the scapegoat

It is tempting to see the 'tragic hero' as a kind of scapegoat for our crimes – or unacted desires. His or her *hybris* attracts the hostility (*phthonos*) of the gods. It allows them to expend on a single figure their need to punish and assert their power over us. The tragic hero is a sacrifice, a means of appeasing the forces that rule the world and keeping at bay the fears they inspire in us. From this point of view, tragedy would be drawing on the kind of rituals that anthropologists have studied in the stories and practices of so-called primitive societies: specifically, rites to do with purification, with expulsion of the unclean, the improper, the alien, or simply the excessive. This might be a partial explanation for the role of tragic characters such as Oedipus, Hippolytus, and

Coriolanus. Their suffering, expulsion, or death helps to purge their communities, a form of *katharsis*. He or she takes the blame, as we say, and in the process saves the rest of us, who like Horatio are left behind in this harsh world to draw our breath in pain (*Hamlet*, V. ii. 300) – and relief.

The difficulty with this theory is that we meet so many different kinds of scapegoat in tragedy, often more than one in the same play. Scapegoats are meant to solve problems of guilt and innocence, but in tragedy they raise questions about the process of judgement by which blame is affixed and punishment executed. What is the difference between a victim and a scapegoat? Are all victims in some sense scapegoats? Some scapegoats are certainly innocent victims, like the Iphigeneia who is sacrificed to the goddess Artemis so the Greek fleet can sail to Troy, or the little boy Astyanax in *Trojan Women* who is sacrificed to the Greeks' fear and hatred of his father Hector. But what of figures less passively led like lambs to the slaughter, characters such as Sophocles' Antigone or Corneille's Polyeucte? We are more inclined to call them martyrs than scapegoats because they suffer for something they positively believe in, and are prepared to die for. Isn't it an insult to call a martyr *tragic*?

The easiest scapegoats are those who do not or cannot speak for themselves, like real goats, lambs, or oxen who cannot reason with their executioners or ask difficult questions. But in tragedy this is just what human scapegoats do. In Aeschylus' *Agamemnon* Iphigeneia is bound and gagged like an animal, but she still manages to 'speak' with her eyes, which pierce the onlookers with pity (240–1). In tragedy the sacrificial victims do get to speak, often with great eloquence – the Euripidean Iphigeneia (in Aulis), for example. Not that they always protest against their fates. In Euripides' *Hecuba*, when the ghost of Achilles demands a blood-sacrifice Polyxena submits to her doom with such grace and dignity that she shames her Greek executioners. So too does Alcestis, who offers to die in place of her husband Admetus, and seems really to do so until Heracles brings her back from the dead. Other victims protest, like the sons of Medea whose dreadful cries off stage we hear as she prepares to murder them. Or the innocent wives in the teeth of unjust accusation, Desdemona in *Othello* and Hermione in *The Winter's Tale*. One of the most memorable is the poet Cinna in *Julius Caesar* who just happens to be in the wrong place at the wrong time. He is torn apart by the mob simply because he has the same name as one of the conspirators: 'It is no matter, his name's Cinna. Pluck but his name out of his heart, and turn him going' (III. iii. 33–4).

If the death of Cinna by random mass violence strikes a special chord for modern audiences, so too should the fate of Queen Elizabeth's Secretary of State, William Davison, in Friedrich Schiller's *Mary Stuart* (1800). Elizabeth has been riven with doubt over what to do about her Catholic rival. The country is being infiltrated by secret agents and terrorists. There are strong arguments for and against executing Mary, but eventually Elizabeth signs the death warrant and summons poor Davison, to whom she entrusts the lethal piece of paper. What is he supposed to do with it? To see the warrant carried out, or to keep it safely locked up? Foreseeing the role in which she's casting him, he pleads with her to tell him her 'will', but she just says, 'Do your job'. She's secured her alibi – and fall-guy. Sure enough, after Mary is executed on what turns out too late to be false evidence, Elizabeth summons Davison to take the blame: 'Wretched man! Is this how you obey my clearest orders?' she rails. And Davison is hauled off to the Tower, a prophetic victim of the deviousness of modern politics. Here and in the *Wallenstein* trilogy (1799) Schiller extends the vision of Shakespeare's history plays to reveal the complexity of agency, motive, and responsibility in a modern world where power has become distributed into networks more vast than Sophocles or Shakespeare knew.

Yet it's as characteristic of their tragedies as of Schiller's that judgement should become more difficult as the play progresses. At the end of *Julius Caesar*, Mark Antony praises the dead Brutus as 'the noblest Roman of them all' (V. v. 67). But what does 'noble' mean? Words of praise and blame that we normally take for granted become opaque, difficult, even unintelligible. In *Hippolytus*, for instance, the word connoting prudence, chastity, self-control, restraint (*sōphrosynē*), becomes ever more mysterious as the play proceeds. No wonder that characters feel like putting all the blame on the gods, or giving them all the credit. On hearing the news that Cornwall has been killed by the servant who couldn't bear to see Gloucester's eyes being put out, Albany exclaims: 'This shows you are above, / You justicers' (*King Lear*, IV. ii. 46—7). On hearing the news that Macbeth has had his wife and family murdered, Macduff asks: 'Did heaven look on / And would not take their part?' (IV. iii. 225-6).

We need to distinguish between the judgements passed by characters within the world of the play, and judgements passed by us, as readers and spectators outside it. Tragedy makes it hard for us to remain impartial analysts and observers. This aggravates the philosophers and moralists and theorists from Plato onwards. They complain about the wiliness of art which draws us into situations we should be trying to judge, inflaming our passions and sympathies, whether it's for the victims and against the injurers, or – a darker thought – luring us into identifying with the infliction of pain, or acquiescing in habits of mind that would perpetuate it. When we read or see a tragedy performed, we participate in the process of 'blame'. We are cast as judges.

But tragedy also asks us to observe the ways in which people reach judgements about who is to blame: the pressures they are under, the motives that impel them, the satisfactions they seek. It offers up for inspection and analysis, not so much the objects themselves, the scapegoats, as the process of scapegoating. Tragedy is interested in the verbs that philosophers want to turn into nouns. As readers and spectators we are invited to think about this juridical, punitive process. Not that tragedy makes us feel we are all to blame, and certainly not equally to blame. It is rather that we are connected, even interconnected, by complex systems of cause and consequence, in which questions of innocence and guilt are all caught up and embroiled, and from which no one should expect to be exempted.

Chapter 5
Big ideas

Trumpet calls

Shortly after George Eliot's death in 1880, F. W. H. Myers recalled walking with her in the gardens of Trinity College Cambridge in the gloom of the day:

> she, stirred somewhat beyond her wont, and taking as her text the three words which have been used so often as the inspiring trumpet-calls of men, – the words, *God*, *Immortality*, *Duty*, – pronounced, with terrible earnestness, how inconceivable was the *first*, how unbelievable the *second*, and yet how peremptory and absolute the *third*. Never, perhaps, have sterner accents affirmed the sovereignty of impersonal and unrecompensing Law.

No Father, Son, and Holy Ghost; no faith, hope, and charity. A ruined trinity for a godless age, with just one survivor.

One can think of other trumpet calls that have inspired men, such as *Liberté, égalité, fraternité*, or Othello's 'Pride, pomp, and circumstance of glorious war!' (III. iii. 359). They do not always come in threes, and they are not always so ringingly named. In the *Iliad*, Achilles and Hector are inspired by *timē* or honour, while for the heroes and heroines in Corneille and Racine it is *gloire* ('name and fame'), and in Ibsen it is the mysterious 'call ot the ideal'. Whatever the words, they invariably contain an idea of justice, and of an absolute obligation to it, as of something inescapably owed to ourselves or others – or god knows what.

In 1917 President Woodrow Wilson addressed the US Congress thus:

> It is a fearful thing to lead this great peaceful people into war, into the most terrible and disastrous of all wars, civilization itself seeming to be in the balance. But the right is more precious than peace, and we shall fight for the things which we have always carried nearest our hearts – . . .

Is peace normal and war an aberration? Homer and Thucydides would not have thought so. Of course men have to fight (and women?). The question is what they are prepared to risk their lives for. An idea called 'the right'? Or more tenderly, closer to home, 'the things which we have always carried nearest our hearts'? But what are these 'things'?

Tragedies have their fair share of inspiring trumpet calls, though what they inspire is often terror – the trumpet of doom or even the Last Trump. We who are not yet going to our doom are left to wonder at Sophocles' Antigone and Ajax, at Shakespeare's Brutus and Coriolanus, at Ibsen's Hedda Gabler and Lorca's Yerma, at the bloody determination with which they cling fast to their right, the one they carry nearest their hearts. But is their right *the* right? What else breeds about their hearts? Tragedies ask questions about the things people are ready to die for. Like the Hamlet who wonders at Fortinbras and his twenty thousand men, fired up by the battlefield's trumpet calls and hurling themselves towards death, 'for a fantasy and trick of fame' (IV. iv: add. passage J, 52). Judge Brack strikes a sardonic note when he rings down the curtain on Hedda Gabler's suicide: 'People just don't do things like that'. But they do, they do.

Myers makes George Eliot with her big idea about Duty sound like a character in a tragedy, a melancholy Sibyl. Writing about *Antigone* in 1856, before embarking on her career as a novelist, Eliot spoke more truly in her own voice about the way tragedy opens up big ideas to reveal the fissures within them. Sophocles' play dramatizes a passionate conflict between duties, rights, claims, principles, loyalties. No single word is sufficient for the grip that ideas exert on the beings who hold them, for the passion with which they hold fast to them – not just Antigone, who fights for the rights of the family, and Creon, who contends for the rights of the city, but Haemon, the lover and son, and Ismene, the sister and niece, both riven between the woman they love and the man to whom they owe obedience. Eliot speaks of 'that struggle between elemental tendencies and established laws by which the outer life of man is gradually and painfully being brought into harmony with his inward needs'. But the inward needs include the force of 'invincible *Erōs*' of which the chorus sing (781–800), and all the elemental tendencies, whether we call them divine or daemonic, that can never be wholly absorbed into 'the outer life of man'.

Hegel and conflict

Eliot is reflecting the absorption of big ideas from the German philosopher G. W. F. Hegel into the mainstream of thinking about tragedy in the 19th century and beyond. At the heart of Hegel's theory is the notion of conflict, and the possibility of its resolution. We have become so accustomed to seeing tragedy in terms of conflict that it is hard to recognize Hegel's originality. Hegel created a radical shift in the terms of thought about tragedy. It was no longer simply a particular dramatic genre, nor a particular kind of story, to which writers and audiences could affix the label. For Hegel, tragedy was more than the sum of particular plays by Sophocles, Shakespeare, Corneille, and Schiller. It was an Idea of which these particular plays were more or less adequate embodiments. This Idea was not just aesthetic but philosophical, ethical, and theological. Most importantly, it was bound up with a big idea about History as the progress of Spirit (*Geist*) in and through time and space.

Hegel saw tragedy as a way of representing the conflicts suffered by Spirit in its descent into the world, its incarnation. Spirit becomes dispersed into particular forms and figures who represent one aspect of it, one 'right'. Tragedy represents the conflict not of right against wrong – which is melodrama or simply justice – but of right against right. The idea could stop there, but for Hegel and Eliot it is important that this conflict is a necessary phase, no matter how painful, in the cause of historical progress, the onward movement of Spirit. But how does one balance the present pain and the deferred gain? Hegel's was a way of acknowledging the conflict at the heart of tragedy while retaining a faith that it was ultimately purposive. It is his emphasis on harmony, resolution, and reconciliation that remains problematic. The idea that the pain and violence of conflict can be justified by the harmony to which it leads may have powerful religious beliefs to support it. Thus St Paul, assuring the Romans that 'the sufferings of this present time are not worthy to be compared with the glory which shall be revealed to us' (*Epistle to the Romans*, 8. 18). But to what terrible abuse can the promise of heaven be put by those in positions of power, not to mention the threat of hell?

The great contribution that Hegel makes to our thinking about tragedy is that he focuses attention on the values that people are prepared to die for. Hegel names some of the forms these can take, though it is noticeable that he selects those that appeal to his moral sense and command his highest respect. These are objective, impersonal, or trans-personal goods that entail binding obligations: love between kith and kin, husband and wife, parent and child, and loyalty to city, state, or political community. Sophocles' *Antigone* was for him a supreme embodiment of just such a clash of rights, between the claims of 'family' and 'state'.

Roman history provided many further such models of tragic collision, as, for example, the story of Lucius Junius Brutus, the Republican hero to whom Shakespeare's near-namesake (Marcus Junius Brutus) looks back. The earlier Brutus avenged the rape of Lucrece and expelled the tyrannical Tarquins. He confirmed his loyalty to the new Republic when he had his two sons executed for joining the attempted counter-revolution. In the turbulent years of the French Revolution and its aftermath, such models had a dangerous relevance. (Hegel lived through these years, being born in 1770 and dying in 1831.) In 1789 Jacques-Louis David painted the dramatic moment when the two sons' bodies are returned to the shattered family. The scene is split between the gloomily adamant father with the twisting feet and the radiant, agonized mother and daughters (Figure 9). This is not necessarily the best way of enlisting new recruits to your political mission, or inducing faith in historical progress.

9. Loyalties that tear us apart

Hegel's view of what constitutes a right works better for some tragedies than others. He is not eager to acknowledge the value of forces that serve morally dubious ends. These too can be rights in the sense on which tragedy insists, in so far as they make inexorable claims on us, whether we like, approve, and admire them or not: sexual passion, for example. *Hippolytus* and *Bacchae* could never be Hegel's favourite plays. Nor can one imagine him enjoying Wagner's *Tristan and Isolde*, Strindberg's *Miss Julie*, or Tennessee Williams's *Streetcar Named Desire*. There is no basement to Hegel's edifice, no dark cellars or underground vaults. It would take Nietzsche and Freud to provide them.

Tragification

Hegel is the first thinker to produce a fully fledged theory of tragedy. He turns tragedy into Tragedy. Before Hegel, what we have is a less concerted set of ideas, principles, and reflections from philosophers, moralists, and critics from Plato and Aristotle onwards, through St Augustine and the Church Fathers to Chaucer's modest description of it as 'a certeyn storie', to Renaissance and neoclassical critics from Scaliger, Minturno, Castelvetro, and Sidney to Corneille, Dryden, and Dr Johnson.

Hegel does not entirely break with the traditional defence against the accusations of Plato and his anti-tragical descendants, in that he continues to stress the inner drive through tragic conflict to a higher coherence. But in the emphasis he lays on the notion of conflict itself, he is putting centre stage the dark secret that Aristotle and others had tried to suppress, and that others after him would develop and revel in, most notably Nietzsche. For in an important sense, Plato was right. Tragedy is dangerous. There *is* rivalry between the philosopher and the tragedian. Tragedy is suspicious of the big ideas the philosopher seeks to promote. Where philosophy abstracts, tragedy particularizes. To adapt the philosopher Margaret Olivia Little, writing about 'particularism', tragedy could be said to dethrone generalizations even if it does not exile them.

For all the service that Hegel does in exposing the centrality of conflict, his attempts to assimilate tragedy into his larger philosophical ambitions make him in turn its rival and antagonist. Similar things could be said of many thinkers since Hegel who have sought to annex tragedy to their visions of the world, or to find in an Idea of Tragedy a substitute for theological and metaphysical schemes that no longer command general assent. In the 19th century there is Arthur Schopenhauer, Søren Kierkegaard, Friedrich Nietzsche; in the 20th, Georg Lukács, Jean-Paul Sartre, Karl Jaspers, George Steiner, René Girard, and many others.

But although Hegel shifts the terms of the debate by creating a case for tragedy's respectability at a more philosophical level than ever before, the tradition of hostility to tragedy continues up to the present day. Now the antagonism comes not so much from the conservative positions espoused by Plato and his followers as from their political opponents, or to put it in crude modern terms, not from the Right but from the Left. There have been exceptions, in the work of Raymond Williams and Terry Eagleton, for example. But in general it has been one of the Left's complaints for the last hundred years that the establishment has hijacked tragedy and turned it into a lackey of the status quo. For Brecht, tragedy had become corrupted into Tragedy, a set of baneful convictions about the inevitability of suffering, an obstacle to political progress. The philosopher Theodor Adorno agreed with him in assailing the idea he believed tragedy promoted, 'that suffering has some higher meaning or that the infinite shines forth in the demise of the finite'. He went on to propose: 'It may be more correct to say that all art is sad than it is to say that it is tragic.' Tragedy turns us into fatalists. Or in the words of Roland Barthes:

> Tragedy is only a way of assembling human misfortune, of subsuming it, and thus of justifying it by putting it into the form of a necessity, of a kind of wisdom, or of a purification.

So down with Hegel, down with Aristotle, and above all down with what the novelist Alain Robbe-Grillet calls 'the systematic *tragification* of the universe'.

Nietzsche's Dionysus

But perhaps these self-styled enemies of tragedy are actually its friends. Perhaps they are attacking a corruption of tragedy, and calling for one of its prime constituents to be restored, its power to question 'higher meanings', 'necessity', 'wisdom'. We do find big ideas in tragedy (and sometimes vice versa), but they are ideas embodied in action. If we think of tragedy not as the expression of an idea of the world but a forum for debating ideas about the world, then the enmity between tragedy and philosophy begins to dissolve. Not all philosophy is tragic, but all tragedy must be in its own particular way – by setting ideas at loggerheads – philosophic.

The philosopher who opens the way to appreciating the role of ideas in tragedy is Nietzsche. In *The Birth of Tragedy* (first published in 1872), Nietzsche sees in ancient Greek drama the collision of fundamentally opposed principles: he calls them Dionysus and Apollo. They have antecedents in Schopenhauer's 'Will' and 'Representation' (*Wille* is the equivalent of Dionysus and *Vorstellung* of Apollo), but what is new is the jubilant approval Nietzsche extends to the Dionysiac principle. This is in stark contrast to Schopenhauer, for whom the Will is the root of all evil, pain, and suffering. For Nietzsche pain is an inevitable corollary of the Life-Force, and as such it is to be welcomed rather than lamented. To put it succinctly: for Schopenhauer pain means death-throes, for Nietzsche pain means birth-pangs. And it is this violence, pain, and conflict that Nietzsche insists is essential to ancient Greek culture. This is a far cry from the 'serenity' (*heiterkeit*) about which his philhellenic predecessors, including Hegel and Matthew Arnold, had waxed lyrical.

Nietzsche tries to be fair to Apollo, but the thrust of his writing is towards celebration of Dionysus, who is at once creator and destroyer, the force behind form, or better, the force that drives *through* all forms, making and unmaking them, including all human artefacts. Apollo is the name for the contrary principle that gives form to force. Apollo individuates and differentiates. Apollo presides over structure, over limits and contours and shapes; Dionysus presides over the process of generation that makes forms possible, but also perpetually dissolves them. The critic A. D. Nuttall remarks that Nietzsche *ought* to have argued that tragedy dramatizes the death of Apollo. Tragedy is a means of celebrating this force of creative dissolution. And Nietzsche locates the source of this joyous acclamation in the chorus, originally the chorus of satyrs or nature beings, through whom is expressed '[T]he metaphysical solace . . . that, despite every phenomenal change, life is at bottom indestructibly joyful and powerful.' This is a massively inflated and original interpretation of the 'pleasure' that tragedy affords us. It makes Aristotle's idea of *katharsis* look puny and pallid by comparison.

When Nietzsche wrote *The Birth of Tragedy*, he imagined Richard Wagner as a modern Dionysus, and – to switch theologies – he imagined himself as John the Baptist to Wagner's Christ. Wagner/Dionysus/Christ was a liberator, deliverer, conqueror; and tragedy was, to borrow a famous phrase from W. B. Yeats, 'a drowning and breaking of the dykes'. But there was another way of understanding tragedy latent in this early work of Nietzsche's. This conceives of tragedy not as celebration but as admonition, punishment, and critique. Left to its own devices the Apollonian principle will tend to ever-increasing rigidity, and the more rigid the form into which it congeals, the more violent will be the revenge of the Dionysiac when it comes to shatter it, as it inevitably will. This can be understood as a recurring psychological rhythm, both at an individual and a collective level. That is, it expresses a truth about the fragility of all human structures, both of individual identity and social institution. The more rigidly resistant to change, the more dangerously liable to violent rupture. Think of the very idea of patriarchy embodied in *King Lear*, for instance. If you resist 'Dionysus', then he, she, it, they will take their revenge. This line of thought characterizes tragedy as a means of conducting a radical critique of human products, structures, and artefacts, of all the things in which we put excessive faith.

This stress plays a subsidiary role in *The Birth of Tragedy*, but it anticipates what will become a major emphasis in Nietzsche's later writings – *The Genealogy of Morals* (1887), for example. It connects up more profitably with other ways of thinking about tragedy that might initially seem at odds with the voluble panegyric of the early work. The later Nietzsche turns a witheringly suspicious eye on the uninspected pretensions of civilization. He identifies 'culture' as something which has been bought at a terrible price, built upon the repression and sublimation of instinct. He unmasks the pathology behind all the self-denying virtues that culture has agreed to praise. 'How much blood and horror lies behind all "good things"!' This could be Freud. It could also be Marx, or a post-Freudian Marxist such as Walter Benjamin, whose most often quoted saying runs: 'There is no document of civilization which is not at the same time a document of barbarism.' *The Birth of Tragedy* is for Nietzsche a prelude in that he casts himself as a herald of Dionysus. In his later writings he takes the starring role himself.

Pain

Wagner's Tristan and Isolde drown supremely in the ecstasy of dissolution. With her final words Isolde soars aloft and disappears in *höchste Lust*, highest pleasure. In tragedy we more frequently hear the despairing cry uttered by Shakespeare's Clarence, who has dreamt of his imminent death: 'Oh Lord! methought what pain it was to drown' (*Richard III*, I. iv. 21). With some help from Schopenhauer, Nietzsche's account of tragedy reintroduces the pain that is missing from Hegel's. For it is the relation between pain and our ideas about it that tragedy seeks to explore. The deceptive preposition 'about' covers a wide range of possibilities:

ideas that cause pain, ideas to which pain gives rise, ideas that seek to justify, interpret, alleviate, and dispel it. William James suggests how:

> all dumb or anonymous psychic states . . . if recognized at all have been named after the substantive perception they led up to, as thoughts 'about' this object or 'about' that, the stolid word *about* engulfing all their delicate idiosyncrasies in its monotonous sounds.

All experience resists being turned into ideas, though less of our experience is exempt from ideas than we like to think. But pain is particularly testing to our powers of rational articulation. '*Deinon gar oude rhēton*': it is a terrible thing that cannot be put into words, says Philoctetes of the pain he suffers (756). It is unspeakable. Pain attacks our very identity; it drives us out of our wits; in pain we are beside ourselves. 'For there was never yet philosopher / That could endure the toothache patiently' (*Much Ado*, V. i. 35–6). A comic over-statement to be sure, but one that expresses the weakness of the spirit when assailed by the weakness of the flesh. Yet it is not so much my pain or yours with which tragedy is concerned. That's our business. It is *the pain of others*, and the painful questions to which this gives rise: such as 'whose business is it?'

This is why we should attend closely to the way within tragedies that people witness each other's pain. To us, the readers, spectators, and viewers, they are third persons, as we are to them, separated by the frame of fiction. Tragedies abound with bystanders, advisors, and counsellors. They hazard all sorts of ideas about what the pain they are witnessing means, what it is for, how and why it has come to pass. There are the choruses of Greek tragedy, whose hymns range through the vocabulary of myth to find one that will explain what is happening here and now in this particular case. If only they could find the right model, example, or precedent, they would be able to 'place' Antigone, Oedipus, Phaedra, Heracles. From their perspective, nothing is more threatening than uniqueness. At other moments, especially in their closing tags, the chorus relapse into commonplace, into moral platitudes and banalities. Individual characters can express these ideas, big and small, as when, for example, Sophocles' Heracles puzzles out the pattern that Zeus has composed for his life and rises to the insight – in Ezra Pound's daring version: 'what / SPLENDOUR, / IT ALL COHERES'. (Though Hegel must have hated all the sex and violence in this play, *Women of Trachis*, he would have approved of this exultant affirmation.) Lacking the chorus, Shakespeare shares out the expression of 'ideas' amongst his whole cast from the prince to the grave-digger.

10. **Justice and torture**

In Titian's great painting, *The Flaying of Marsyas* (Figure 10), a very youthful Apollo is kneeling to skin the flesh off the satyr who challenged him to a musical contest, and lost, as everyone does who challenges the gods. Marsyas is also surprisingly young, a bemused peasant boy being crucified upside down, his goat-legs strung shamefully aloft. The painting is crowded with other figures: two of the god's servants on the left, two fellow-satyrs on the right; two dogs, one foolish and shameful, lapping the blood, the other nobly restrained. Most important of all is the figure on the losing side who balances the punishing god (if punishing is indeed what he's doing). This is King Midas in the pose of the thinker, the melancholy, pensive philosopher. It may well be a self-portrait of the artist. Amongst Renaissance thinkers the myth of Marsyas was frequently interpreted as an allegory of the triumph of light over darkness, spirit over flesh, celestial over bestial, ordering harmony over chaotic impulse, and so on.

Big ideas indeed. Titian's painting certainly refers to them and puts them in play. But it also gives the most vivid embodiment to Marsyas's pain and perplexity. This painful perplexity is passed on to the philosophic spectator, who represents both the artist and the viewer, as we all try to figure it out. The idea that would make such good sense of the pain being that what we saw was no longer torture but justice.

Chapter 6
No laughing matter

Derision

When Chaucer's Troilus is slain, he ascends to the eighth sphere and looks back down with contempt on 'this litel spot of erthe', 'this wrecched world', 'the blynde lust, the which that may nat laste'. It is 'al vanite' by comparison with 'the pleyn felicite / That is in hevene above'. As for the grief of those who mourn his death, it makes him laugh. This puts us in an odd position. It seems a bit unfeeling of Troilus to abandon the earthly misery he's been enduring until just a moment ago. Suddenly he's a stranger, as carefree as the gods on that vase depicting the death of Hippolytus (Figure 7). Readers are always half in and half out of the fiction, but Troilus's laughter puts us on the spot. Do we laugh with him up there or grieve with the mourners down here?

Comedy's more than a barrel of laughs; there's more to tragedy than tears. We weep for joy, and we laugh for all sorts of good and bad reasons – sardonically, maliciously, nervously, sociably, heartily, triumphantly, insanely. If the brute matter of tragedy consists of pain, grief, death, and bereavement, laughter raises difficult questions about the distance from which we view it. 'Lord, what fools these mortals be!' exclaims Puck (*A Midsummer Night's Dream*, III. ii. 115). From the safety of another world, human antics may well seem hilarious, and much laughter in art encourages us to view suffering in this unfeeling, even heartless way, as a matter for de-rision – which literally means laughing *down* at someone or something – as if we were gods or angels or spirits, or simply superior beings. As Troilus now is.

'Tragedy is not disaster. It is a disaster when a cartwheel goes over a frog, but it is not a tragedy', says D. H. Lawrence. Only a child or a fool would grieve for a flattened frog. A dearly loved dog or cat might be different. But can the death of an animal ever be *tragic*? Let us keep things, as we say, in proportion. 'Comedy is tragedy that happens to *other* people', writes Angela Carter. Mel Brooks's version is funnier because more elaborate: 'Tragedy is when I cut my finger. Comedy is when *you* walk into an open sewer and die.' Heartless humour protects us from having our hearts excessively or unnecessarily taxed.

> Weep not for little Léonie
> Abducted by a French Marquis!
> Though loss of honour was a wrench
> Just think how it's improved her French.

Harry Graham's *Ruthless Rhymes for Heartless Homes* (1899) would have appealed to the Oscar Wilde who remarked, of the death of Dickens's Little Nell in the *The Old Curiosity Shop*, that one would need a heart of stone to read it without laughing. 'The comic', says Henri Bergson, 'demands something like a momentary anesthesia of the heart.'

Can anything be turned to laughter? Even something as clearly tragic (surely) as the tale of Oedipus? There is certainly a long tradition of mocking the solemnity of tragedy from Aristophanes onwards, including a (post-classical) genre intriguingly known as *hilarotragōdia*. This would be a good description of the play put on by Bottom and his colleagues for Theseus and his courtiers at the end of *A Midsummer Night's Dream*, 'Pyramus and Thisbe' – tragedy hilarified. There's a good case for laughing at the

11. Is this a dagger which I see before me?

pretensions of tragedy when it's not the real thing. Whether the travesty of *Macbeth* in James Gillray's cartoon (Figure 11) is bad acting or deliberate farce, it's hard to tell. To Parisian audiences in 1822, nourished on the neoclassical scorn of Voltaire for English barbarism, *Othello* seemed ridiculous. An English journal indignantly reported that 'Desdemona was put to bed and smothered amid roars of laughter.' Is nothing sacred? The physical violence in Mel Gibson's film *The Passion of the Christ* (2004) has tempted at least one viewer to confess that he had to seek refuge in laughter.

Does it *all* depend on how it's told?

> There once lived a man called Oedipus Rex
> You may have heard about his odd complex
> His names appears in Freud's index
> 'Cos he – loved his mother.

Thus Tom Lehrer's heartlessly cheerful version, delightfully ignoring the obvious rhyme-word. Do you have to be a safe distance from the disaster before you can laugh at it, like the patrician lovers at the end of *A Midsummer Night's Dream*? Or is laughter a means to creating or claiming that distance? This is certainly the case with what we call 'gallows-humour', such as Mercutio famously wields as he jests his way to death: 'Ask for me to-morrow, and you shall find me a grave man' (*Romeo and Juliet*, III. i. 97–8). Challenged by the girl he thinks he loves to entertain the terminally ill for a year, Berowne (Biron) asks incredulously:

> To move wild laughter in the throat of death? –
> It cannot be, it is impossible.
> Mirth cannot move a soul in agony.
>
> (*Love's Labour's Lost*, V. ii. 842–4)

But mirth might be a means of escaping the agony, your own and others', even just for a moment.

We can laugh down at frogs and other small creatures, belittling their catastrophes. We can also laugh up at the heavens, in heroic resistance. This is what we mean by laughing something 'to scorn', whether it's the triumphant contempt of the torturer or the desperate defiance of the victim. This is the satanic laughter described by the poet Charles Baudelaire when he reflects on the doomed outcasts who defy God in Romantic drama and Gothic fiction. Byron's poetry and drama are full of them, and so is 19th-century grand opera. Verdi's Iago would be a good example, in his *Otello*. Without the support of music, such figures can easily seem 'operatic', teetering on the edge of the absurd and ripe for parody.

Comic relief

It has often been said that laughter provides tragedy with 'comic relief'. This is a way of thinking about the satyr play that followed the performance of three tragedies in ancient Athens. After the rigours of tragedy, the explosion of ribald, carnival humour and fantasy was the audience's reward. And though it is anachronistic to use the word 'carnival', the connotations are pertinent. They point to the fleshly pleasures that compensate for the impositions of discipline, austerity, renunciation. The release of laughter, hilarity, 'fun' helps to make the pain bearable. It distracts us from the ordeal of the protagonists at the centre of the action, Christ on the cross or Lear on his 'wheel of fire'. We may think of the jocularity of 'low' characters like the Sentry in Sophocles' *Antigone*; of the facetiousness of the soldiers nailing Christ to the cross in the medieval Mystery cycles; of the jests and japes of all the low-life in Shakespeare from the Nurse in *Romeo and Juliet* to the Fool in *King Lear*, the grave-diggers in *Hamlet* to the Porter in *Macbeth*.

This is fine as far as it goes, the idea that they offer a 'sense of proportion': don't be so solemn, don't take yourself or the world so seriously. Such ultra-earthly common sense is remarkably consonant with Troilus's other-worldly, celestial wisdom. As Plato says: 'no human affairs are worth great trouble'. This can pass rather easily into the mouths of authority figures who dispense what they think is 'good counsel', like Friar Laurence consoling Juliet's parents with the thought that 'nature's tears are reason's merriment' (*Romeo and Juliet*, IV. iv. 110), or Gertrude advising her son, young Hamlet, that 'all that lives must die, / Passing through nature to eternity' (I. ii. 72–3).

But the phrase 'comic relief' will not suffice if we think of it as mere distraction. This vital component of dramatic form complicates the rhythmic experience of the play in performance and the angles from which the audience reads it. Most drama, except the very short, retains our attention by variations of tempo, mood, texture, focus, or perspective, for which the implied analogies with music and the visual arts are helpful. As a local effect, a comic voice or scene assists the whole rhythm by heightening and lowering tension. Think of the big public scenes of confrontation in Shakespeare where everyone is on their mettle and guard: Othello, Desdemona, and

Brabantio in front of the Venetian senate, for example (I. iii). Then all the grandees sweep off and leave us alone with the servants, retainers, and hangers-on – in this case Iago and Roderigo. A lot of the comedy in Shakespearean tragedy (and history plays) derives from this apparent relief from the inexorability of 'plot'. It's easier to breathe in an air of loose talk, down-to-earth, unbuttoned, when Iago or Falstaff or Mercutio or Hamlet or Enobarbus seems to be just passing the time.

But this is deceptive, because the plays they feature in turn out *not* to be comedies. The plot and the plotting go on and no one is exempt from it; indeed, Iago is working on it all the time (and we are complicit with him). Relief, respite, escape: this is not what the comic voice in tragedy is most importantly for. 'I am nothing if not critical', says Iago (II. i. 119), and in this he is closely akin to the other figures just named. They play a vital part in questioning the ambitions of those around them, their elevated language, their high ideals, their lofty sense of themselves, the Othellos, Hotspurs, Romeos, Antonies. Think of Mercutio on 'love' (*Romeo and Juliet*, II. i. 3–42, II. iii. 1–92), or Falstaff on 'honour' (*I Henry IV*, V. i. 127–40). This is comedy with an edge and laughter with a bite. Othello rightly claims he has done the state some service, but so too in their way do Iago, Lear's Fool, and Cleopatra's clown.

Not all tragedy finds a place for laughter. It has a certain presence in some Greek tragedies, especially in Euripides, where the humour can be distinctly 'black', as we have learned to call it. As, for example, in *Bacchae*, when Pentheus appears in drag, primping and preening before Dionysus (912–76). This laughter is close to terror and horror, as it is in *Macbeth*. But there is no laughter in Seneca or Racine or Wagner's *Tristan and Isolde*. This has something to do with the place of the body in their drama. If the body is acknowledged at all – and it is still not certain whether Seneca's dramas were designed for performance – then it is flesh that must be transcended by spirit. This is why the rare moments when Racine's characters sit down are so dramatic. And that is why

W. H. Auden complains, in a distinctly English idiom, that 'It is impossible to imagine any of Racine's characters sneezing or wanting to go to the bathroom, for in his world there is neither weather nor nature.' Nor laughter. French classical tragedy is, says Auden, 'another planet'.

First time tragedy, second time farce?

Hegel said that important historical events and characters occur twice. To which Marx cleverly added – first time tragedy, second time farce. This might be an explanation for modern tragedy, and why it's just not the real thing any more. Instead of heroes, we have hospital cases, madmen, and clowns. The bourgeois Louis Napoleon who prompted Marx to his *mot* simply didn't have the stature of Napoleon Bonaparte, his tragic predecessor. Now tragedy always belongs to the past, so the argument goes. The vertical scale on which it depended, the heights and depths on which an Oedipus or a Faust or a Bonaparte could perch, from which he could topple – they're gone. The world has been flattened; everyone's equal, nobody's different, so no particular death (or life) can be distinguished from any other. So of course modern literature spawns a new breed of characters who protest against their own mediocrity, who insist on climbing and diving, up mountains and down to the depths – characters who *want to be tragic*. They want stories to give their weightless lives the gravity and dignity conferred by the most prestigious of literary genres: like Masha in Chekhov's *The Seagull*, who stalks round in black telling people that she's in mourning for her life, or Hamm in Beckett's *Endgame* with his ridiculous scraps of old tragic rhetoric. From Ibsen and his contemporaries onwards, what we get is at worst pseudo-tragedy, or at best the diagnosis of a condition in which real tragedy is no longer possible. It is this sense of bereavement that drives characters to try and repeat – in vain – the heroic ordeals suffered by an Antigone, a Hamlet, a Faust, a Napoleon. According to this view, modern tragedy exists only in pathological forms as nostalgia, as the compulsion to repeat, as farce.

But this is not the whole truth about repetition. The factory worker required to repeat a single small task might have something more to say about it. So too might other labourers, such as the heroine of Hardy's *Tess of the D'Urbervilles*, who is given some philosophical thoughts about identity. They are a bit startling, not least to her admirer Angel Clare, who does not expect a simple country milkmaid to have read Schopenhauer or Darwin. At one point in their courting, Angel asks Tess if she'd like to embark on further education, history for example. She says no, not much: 'Sometimes I feel I don't want to know anything more about it than I know already.' Why not?

> Because what's the use of learning that I am one of a long row only – finding out that there is set down in some old book somebody just like me, and to know that I shall only act her part; making me sad, that's all. The best is not to remember that your nature and your past doings have been just like thousands' and thousands', and that your coming life and doings 'll be like thousands' and thousands'.
>
> (ch. 19, 'The Rally')

So she doesn't want to learn anything? 'I shouldn't mind learning why – why the sun do shine on the just and the unjust alike . . . . But that's what books will not tell me.' This is what it's like to *feel* you are a copy – not a leaf, a statistic, or just another country milkmaid viewed from a distance, but imagined from the inside. The answer is that it hurts. It's this pain that we need to hold on to as we think about the possibilities of modern tragedy.

Just a few years after Hardy's *Tess*, the French philosopher Henri Bergson published an important book about laughter (*Le Rire*). Bergson's theory of comedy depends on repetition. He proposes that we laugh at human beings when they behave with mindless automatism, when they lose their power to originate or improvise or simply choose – in a word, when they start repeating themselves. This certainly seems to be true of the characters in Chekhov's plays and stories, written around the same time. In *The Three Sisters*,

Vershinin wonders 'what it would be like if we could start living all over again, knowing exactly what we were doing . . . . Then we'd all try hard not to repeat ourselves, I imagine.' It's so hard to avoid repeating yourself – or other people. There are all sorts of repetition and mimicry and copying in *The Three Sisters*. Masha quotes Pushkin. Solyony quotes Krylov and pretends to be Lermontov. Chebutykin copies things from the newspapers. At one point in Act II, he is reading the newspaper and says out of the blue: 'Balzac got married in Berdichev.' And he writes it down in his notebook. Irene is playing patience, overhears the words, and in turn repeats them. It is as if words were ballast or buoys that might help to counteract the sense of vertigo, to keep you afloat or stop you floating away.

The most telling repetition in the play is the sisters' yearning cry for the city they long to escape to: 'Moscow, Moscow, Moscow'. They never get there. For many of Chekhov's characters, repetition has a talismanic, even magical quality. The fantasy is that if you repeat words often enough, somehow they will belong to you, or even 'come true'. But repetition achieves nothing, creates nothing, conserves nothing. On the contrary, every time you repeat a word, it loses a little meaning. This is the modern myth of entropy, the idea that energy and meaning are always running down, or never renewing themselves again to the same point.

Vacant possession

Emptiness provides an important point of overlap between comedy and tragedy. It can be a comic relief to discover that where you expected to find something inside, there is nothing – a blank, absence, vacancy. It can equally well be a tragic shock, depending on what you hoped to find there – inside yourself, inside someone else, inside a home or city, of bricks or of words. It can be comically liberating to discover that you are, as Baudelaire says, both *soi et un autre*, yourself and another. It is tragically demoralizing to discover that you are neither one nor the other. The hollow can inspire a sense of comic freedom from the gravity of innerness. What a relief to empty one's innards, as it were, or not to be taxed with confronting someone else's innards. Or it can inspire a sense of tragic lack – just when we expected to grasp the heart of the matter, a core of being, the grail of centrality itself. Comic freedom, or tragic lack.

Bergson's theory of comedy depends on recognizing a kind of emptiness when human beings forget themselves, or their best selves, and behave like animals or machines. The body is deserted by the spirit; it loses its grace and suppleness and becomes rigid, automatic, mechanical. Bergson writes:

> A laughable expression of the face, then, is one that will make us think of something rigid and, so to speak coagulated [*figé*], in the wonted mobility of the face.

But not all facial rigidity is laughable. Some kinds of stillness are dignified because we recognize the power of human will restraining the face's capacity to 'move'. And other kinds of facial stillness are beautiful because of their involuntary freedom from movement. The visual arts – painting, sculpture, photography, and film – are capable of staging such dramatic relations between mobility and rigidity. Bergson anticipates this objection. Of course not all stillness is comic. The beauty and expressiveness of stillness, he says, derives from its promise of interiority, of secrecy and mystery; it is for this reason that it is not comic. 'But a comic expression of the face is one that promises nothing more than it gives.'

We know that T. S. Eliot took an interest in Bergson, at least for a while, and we can hear Bergson behind the lines in 'Rhapsody on a Windy Night' that go like this:

> So the hand of the child, automatic,
> Slipped out and pocketed a toy that was running along the quay,
> I could see nothing behind that child's eye.

Eliot was also interested in the most recalcitrant of Shakespeare's tragic protagonists, Caius Martius Coriolanus. Poised on the brink of destroying the city that has banished him, Coriolanus prompts one of his erstwhile fellows to the bitter remark: 'I tell you, he does sit in gold, his eye / Red as 'twould burn Rome' (V. i. 63–4). What is behind his eye? There are readers who confidently affirm that Coriolanus is a hollow man. He has no innards, as Hamlet and Macbeth have. He is what everyone in the play says he is: a machine, an animal, a thing, devoid of human will or volition. According to Bergson, such a creature should be the essence of the comic, and Bergson can help us see what *is* comic about Coriolanus. But he is also terrifying, and what is in the end more tragic than comic about him is the fathomless doubt about what goes on, what could or might go on inside him. At times he can seem the most modern of Shakespeare's tragic creations, precisely because he is ungifted with the powers of self-expression we associate with a Hamlet or Macbeth, let alone the great Sophoclean figures whose selfhood is embodied in the very language that they speak.

Habit

Most suffering is not gorgeous, spectacular, or eloquent. One of the great achievements of the 19th-century realist novel was to find ways of representing apparently ordinary, inevitable forms of suffering and give them the special attention by virtue of which they would strike the reader as extra-ordinary, un-inevitable, and therefore tragic. Tragedy is a way of seeing things, and so is comedy. Ibsen and Chekhov develop ways of putting on stage some of the discoveries of the realist novel. They expose to a hard, derisive light the ways in which people become habituated to pain and misery and suffering. Here's an anecdote from Chekhov's *Notebooks*:

> A shy young man came on a visit for the night: suddenly a deaf old woman came into his room, carrying an enema, and operated on

him. He thought that this must be the usual thing and so did not protest; in the morning it turned out that the old woman had made a mistake.

He thought this must be *the usual thing*? Not protesting because it seems to be the usual thing: this could be a tragic mistake – a distinctly modern version of what Aristotle meant by *hamartia*. Beware of the deaf old woman in the night.

There is nothing, it seems, to which people will not become habituated. First time tragedy, second time farce, third time . . . ? Business as usual, the world as it is, good old realism? Modern tragic art seeks to shock us into thought about the most baneful kinds of repetition in which our lives are swathed. Consider Samuel Beckett's *Play* (1964). Two women and one man face the audience, buried in urns up to their necks. They also face a spotlight which makes them speak when it lights them up. Together they tell the story of their adulterous triangle, the usual thing in all its banality. But they seem oblivious of each other. When their story comes to a kind of conclusion, they go back to the beginning and start again. In reading the play, the effect is difficult and perhaps impossible to gauge. All you get is the laconic stage direction: 'Repeat play'. But in the theatre it is a remarkable experience. The first time round it is funny, and we laugh a lot. The second time there's a hush. When the characters start a third time, we feel a certain panic. Fortunately they stop; or rather the play stops, and the audience is released. But we can imagine the characters going on for ever.

First time tragedy, second time farce? Not always, not necessarily. In his essay 'The Myth of Sisyphus' (1942), Albert Camus reflects on the fate of the man condemned to heave a rock up a hill and watch it roll down again for all eternity. For Camus he is the epitome of 'the absurd hero' who embraces his endless torment in magnificent lucidity, undeceived by hope, undestroyed by despair. Camus writes:

If this myth is tragic, that is because its hero is conscious . . . . The lucidity that was to constitute his torture at the same time crowns his victory. There is no fate that cannot be surmounted by scorn.

Sisyphus in hell, Troilus in heaven: both laughing at tragedy.

Chapter 7
Words, words, words

Breaking silence

Silence can be beautiful, blissful, heroic, agonized, crushing. It all depends whose and when. It also depends on the words and sounds, desired and feared, that we might hear or utter and don't. Think of Cordelia's first words: 'What shall Cordelia speak? Love and be silent' (*King Lear*, I. i. 62). And of the dying Hamlet's last: 'The rest is silence' (V. ii. 310). Most important for tragedy are the silences that greet the hard questions asked by people in pain, as Lear does over his daughter's dead body: 'Why should a dog, a horse, a rat have life, / And thou no breath at all?' (V. iii. 282–3). These silences are not only those of God or the gods, but of all the authorities to whom we look up for 'the answers', and of all the witnesses and bystanders who are lost for words, including ourselves as readers and viewers.

It is actions rather than conditions that are crucial – the act of silencing and being silenced, the refusal to speak, the thwarting of utterance. Near the end of Brian Friel's *Translations* (1981) an English officer strikes a young Irish woman back into the dumbness she had struggled out of in the play's opening moments. In so far as the state of silence is tragic, it is because of the pain that has gone into its making, and the difficulty of finding the right words to break it. We speak of aircraft breaking the sound barrier, but in tragedy it's the silence barriers that are at issue: the frontiers that separate human beings from gods and from beasts, the living from the dead, men from women, old from young, friend from foe, us from them, and so on, endlessly, all 'the others' we just can't hear or refuse to listen to because they 'don't speak the same language' (as with the Irish and English in Friel's *Translations*). All the more painfully, there is the silence that falls between intimate beings who ought to be able to exchange words freely. Some of these silences seem more natural than others, but it's exactly their inevitability that tragedy questions. Words do cross the boundaries; the silence can and should be broken.

In Shakespeare's *Titus Andronicus*, Lavinia is deprived by violence of her hands and her tongue, yet even she can break out of her silence to tell her story. At the climax of Brecht's best play, *Mother Courage and her Children* (1949), the dumb Kattrin finally 'speaks' by beating the drum that warns the besieged citizens of Halle of their impending doom. Then there is that ordinary victim of marital bullying, Shakespeare's Emilia. At last she bravely rebels, at the risk of her life:

> Iago: 'Swounds, hold your peace!
> Emilia: 'Twill out, 'twill out. I peace?
> No, I will speak as liberal as the north.
> Let heaven, and men, and devils, let 'em all,
> All, all cry shame against me, yet I'll speak.
>
> (*Othello*, V. ii. 225—8)

So too, Cornwall's servant, who cannot stand by any longer in silence, and watch Gloucester's eyes being put out (*King Lear*, III. vii. 70–80). Both pay with their lives.

'Breaking the silence' has become a modern way of thinking about tragedy for artists of many different kinds, including historians, journalists, documentary photographers, and film-makers. Tillie

Olsen's influential book *Silences* (first published 1980) is a good example; so is the work of the photographers gathered in the collection *Witness in Our Time* (2000). Once silenced by disadvantages of gender, age, class, and race, some of the victims of history are at last represented, in more than one sense of the word. Liberated, if you like, save that the liberation is also a means of mourning those for whom it has come too late, those left behind.

George Eliot writes with feeling about the suffering that goes unnoticed, unheard, unrecorded.

> for there is much pain that is quite noiseless; and vibrations that make human agonies are often a mere whisper in the roar of hurrying existence.

It is of Dante and Virgil she is thinking when she goes on to say:

> The poets have told us of a dolorous enchanted forest in the under world. The thorn-bushes there, and the thick-barked stems, have human histories hidden in them; the power of unuttered cries dwells in the passionless-seeming branches, and the red warm blood is darkly feeding the quivering nerves of a sleepless memory that watches through all dreams. These things are a parable.

Eliot is rethinking the traditional tragic paradigms of crime and punishment. She is urging a new attention to historical process, and to the pain that is 'noiseless', 'unuttered' – until the artist gives it a voice. She appeals for attention, a kind of silence that will allow the cries of those who have *seemed* silent to be heard. Simone Weil concurs:

> In those who have suffered too many blows, in slaves, for example, that place in the heart from which the infliction of evil evokes a cry of surprise may seem to be dead. But it is never quite dead; it is simply unable to cry out any more. It has sunk into a state of dumb and ceaseless lamentation.

Much of Tony Harrison's poetry addresses the anger and grief aroused by the 'dumb', which they cannot or have not expressed for themselves. 'National Trust' tells of the 'stout upholders of our law and order', who are curious about the possibility of measuring a 'bottomless pit' in Castleton. They borrow a convict for the experiment: 'and winched him down; and back, flayed, grey, mad, dumb': 'Not even a good flogging made him holler!'

But the poet can holler for him. Harrison has been described as 'an avenger speaking for the silent or dispossessed', 'a sort of prole-prince of Elsinore'.

Reticence

Harrison's convict is so far gone that he can't even 'holler', yet this could be a matter for pride and admiration. This is the traditional glory of the Stoic celebrated by Seneca and bequeathed to the early Christian martyrs. The Stoic ideal resurfaces in the Renaissance centuries later. In John Ford's play *The Broken Heart* (1633), Calantha dances on even as she receives news of 'death, and death, and death'. She chooses her own death in her own time with the magnificent avowal: 'They are the silent griefs which cut the heart-strings; / Let me die smiling.' To choose silence is a way of defying pain, as Shakespeare's Iago does when he declares: 'From this time forth I never will speak word' (V. ii. 310). The victim can turn the tables on the oppressor by refusing to cry out, or even to answer at all. Silence may be the expression of sovereign contempt. One of the greatest literary examples is provided by Virgil's Dido. When her lover Aeneas abandons her for his historical mission to found Rome, the Queen of Carthage kills herself. On his journey to the underworld he meets her again and tries to engage her in conversation. Dido listens to him but says never a word and then just turns on her heel (VI. 470–4). 'Perhaps the most telling snub in all poetry', says T. S. Eliot, slightly tarnishing the moment's dignity. Christ's silence before Pontius Pilate is another great model, rather more, you might say, than a 'snub'.

'Give sorrow words', says Malcolm to Macduff (*Macbeth*, IV. iii. 210). The latter has just received the horrific news that in his absence from Scotland his family have been murdered by Macbeth's agents. But how much good do they do, mere words, in the face of irremediable grief? That is, both the words uttered by the person suffering the pain, and the words uttered by those who proffer consolation and explanation: the words that pass between them. This is an important and recurring scene in tragedy. Something terrible happens off stage, and a messenger must bring the bad news to the nearest and dearest. In its purest form, the scene just requires two figures, the one who has to break the news and the one who receives it. Each of these has his or her ordeal to endure: how to put the brute event into words and how to receive it. Sophocles creates an extraordinarily dramatic effect when he gets the listener, after enduring a lengthy speech from the messenger, to exit abruptly in silence. Deianeira in *Women of Trachis*, Eurydice in *Antigone*, and Jocasta in *Oedipus Tyrannus*: they all walk promptly off to their self-inflicted death. The message is sometimes addressed to, and often heard by, more than one person. In Sophocles' *Electra* the (false) news of Orestes' death is delivered to two listeners at one and the same time, his sister Electra and his mother Clytemnestra, but it means very different things to each. This 'extra' figure may be less personally implicated in the news and thus a witness to the principal listener's grief, as the chorus always are in Greek tragedy, or as Malcolm is to Macduff. But it's in the nature of these traumatic scenes that he or she cannot remain a disinterested or uninterested witness. 'Let grief / Convert to anger', counsels Malcolm (IV. iii. 230–1), perhaps prematurely, needing to harness the force of Macduff's turbulent passions.

Nothing can harness the babel that streams out of Beckett's 'Mouth' in his short play *Not I* (1973). This fractured, repetitive narrative is itself a kind of 'messenger speech', in the sense that the mad Ophelia's snatches of speech and song are reports from the chaos of her inner world to a helpless group of bystanders, including her brother Laertes. Beckett's play has only one other figure in the shape of a silent 'Auditor'. Indeed, 'shape' is just what he or she is, 'enveloped from head to foot in loose black djellaba, with hood'. Four times, with diminishing strength, this figure raises its arms 'in a gesture of helpless compassion', at the points when Mouth refuses to admit the first person into speech: ' . . . what? . . who? . . no! . . she!' Until the fifth time there is an added, triumphant 'SHE!' – and no response from Auditor at all.

The greatest tragic artists understand the effect of reticence. Modern readers find it hard to be interested in Seneca's characters because when they suffer a terrible blow, they become instantly and inordinately loquacious. The Renaissance had more sympathy for their elaborate rhetoric. In *Hercules Oetaeus* (part of which is probably spurious), Deianeira is deprived of the eloquently silent exit that Sophocles gives her. Instead she launches into a huge lament accusing herself of the worst of crimes and invoking the most enormous punishments. The same is true of Iole, whom Sophocles makes a wonderfully ominous, because entirely silent, presence. In the Senecan version her monologue is unstoppable. Only music could make this tolerable. (Handel makes a fine oratorio out of it – *Hercules* (1745).) Senecan characters have no need of our sympathies, though they may command our admiration. This is frequently the case in opera, where the listener's imaginative engagement with the fictional character's grief is neutralized by admiration for the brilliance with which it is expressed by composer and performer.

Seneca looks forward to opera, but for the mainstream of European Renaissance drama he provides a model of verbal and emotional excess, of what it's like never to be short of words. This sense of infinite vocal resources derives from Seneca's vision of a limitless cosmos, of human energies unchecked by gods. Hence the resonance of Jason's final lines as Medea soars up and away: *Per alta vade spatia sublimi aethere; / testare nullos esse, qua veheris, deos* ('Travel on high through the lofty spaces of heaven and bear witness that there are no gods where you ride'). Shakespeare takes over this vision of infinity and the language of enormity, but he places the characters to whom he gives it – Othello, Lear, Cleopatra – in a world that *does* have limits, not least the limits of their own physical powers. And he chastens their excess by setting them against other voices, more restrained, more mundane, more circumspect.

The great plays of Corneille and Racine depend on a restraint and constraint through which violence is constantly threatening to erupt. In Figure 12 we get a (literal) glimpse of the murder of Racine's Britannicus, a scene that on stage is only described in words. Half the witnesses run out screaming, says the narrator, Burrhus. *Mais ceux qui de la cour ont un plus long usage / Sur les yeux de César composent leur visage* (V. v. 1625–6): 'But those with more experience of the court keep their eyes fixed on Caesar' – the Emperor Nero, the murderer – 'and compose their expressions accordingly'. Composure, that is the way to survive. When she hears of his death, the woman who loves Britannicus loses control for a moment. *Ah! mon Prince*, Junie exclaims – and instantly apologizes for her 'outburst' (*Transport*, V. iv. 1603–4). In Corneille's *Horace*, Camille has to listen to the lengthy speech describing the death of her betrothed at the hands of her brother, the eponymous hero. Her sole uttered response is the word *Hélas!* (IV. ii. 1123). This leaves space for the spectator to read deep feelings into her such as Seneca never allows. There is an equally effective but more complex *Hélas!* at the very end of Racine's *Bérénice*. The queen is saying a last farewell to the man she has loved and been loved by, the emperor Titus: *Pour la dernière fois, adieu, Seigneur* (V. vii. 1506: 'For the last time, farewell, my lord'). Somebody has to complete the line she's left dangling and conclude the play. But it is not Titus, as Bérénice must wish. Instead, it is uttered by the *other* man in the triangle, Antiochus – whose love for her has never been reciprocated. This communicates a sharp sense of the pain of all three parties to this irreparable moment.

12. Beyond words, in the mind's eye

Speech impediments

What a dream, to be articulate in the midst of passion – anger, desire, grief – yet when we meet it in reality it usually seems specious, a glib and oily artfulness. Great tragic art satisfies our dreams by endowing characters with the verbal resourcefulness we never muster for ourselves, especially when it's expressed through the body and voice of gifted performers, most of all when they exploit the full range of the human voice in song. If only we could speak like Antigone or Heracles, Hamlet or Phèdre, like David Garrick, Laurence Olivier, Ian McKellen, Sarah Siddons, Peggy Ashcroft, or Rachel, or sing like Tristan and Isolde, Otello and Desdemona, like Kirsten Flagstad, Maria Callas, Dietrich Fischer-Diskau, or Placido Domingo. We remember with gratitude lines and passages, turns of phrase and voice, that seem to grasp the shapes of true passion, the moments when for once, amidst all the inequities of tragedy, language appears equal to what it addresses and expresses. We can put up with protracted eloquence in opera or song cycles such as Schubert's *Winterreise*, but we can only do so because we know the enormous demands on the performers. We know they could crack under the strain, or just crack a top note. We know they could 'fail'. Risk is intrinsic to all performance, but where tragedy is concerned the sense of risk is written into the text itself as something to be embodied, encountered, endured by anyone who reads, witnesses, or performs it, no matter how gifted or ham-fisted.

This is why tragedies show the way words fail at critical moments. This is not the only truth that tragedies express, for they also show how words go on, how we go on in the teeth of disaster. It is nonsense to say that there can or should be 'no poetry after Auschwitz', the poet Tony Harrison protests. We should take courage, he argues, from the conviction embodied in the ancient Greek mask with its open eyes and mouth that go on seeing and speaking in the face of catastrophe. One can readily agree with him that tragedy expresses a general faith in the indomitability of the human spirit, but it also honours the mortality of the particular spirits whose flesh and blood fail them. Racine's Titus 'fails' at a critical moment when he can't tell his beloved Bérénice that they must part for ever. They share the magnificent collapse of the line of verse that is eked out between them.

```
T: Mais ...
B:          Achevez.
T:                  Hélas!
B:                        Parlez.
T:                              Rome ... L'empire ...
```

(II. iv. 623)

('But ...' 'Go on.' 'Alas!' 'Speak.' 'Rome ... The Empire ...')
Despairingly, the young emperor turns to his confidant Paulin and they exit, leaving the queen asking in bewilderment what this 'silence' means.

Titus is stammering. This would be a fair way of describing much of the speech that is important to tragedy, when people fail to find the right words. 'Stammering is the native eloquence of us fog people', says the doomed young Edmund Tyrone in Eugene O'Neill's *A Long Day's Journey into Night* (1956). The idea of the fog or mist, the foul and filthy air that chokes speech out of us is a potent one in tragedy, especially in the 'northern' imagination. There is a classic instance of stammering in the most literal sense of the term in Herman Melville's novella *Billy Budd* (1924). Billy the Handsome Sailor, the image of innocent physical strength and beauty, is afflicted with one tragic flaw, and it's this, when he's falsely accused by the villainous Claggart, that prompts him to the 'crime' for which he is hanged. Because he can't get the words out to protest his innocence, his lethal fist shoots out instead and fells the officer stone-dead. In Philip Roth's fine novel *American Pastoral* (1998), the protagonist's daughter Merry Levov lives out at length a comparable fate. Another agonized stammerer is Ben, the Oedipal son in a version of *Hippolytus* set in County

Donegal, Brian Friel's *Living Quarters* (1977). Tony Harrison points to the rage that fires his own work when he appends this as one of the epigraphs to his sonnet sequence 'The School of Eloquence':

> How you became a poet's a mystery!
> Wherever did you get your talent from?
> I say: I had two uncles, Joe and Harry –
> one was a stammerer, the other dumb.

In another poem he writes: 'Articulation is the tongue-tied's fighting.'

Beyond the scream

Hamlet's last word may be 'silence'. But in the Folio text of the play, it is followed by 'O, o, o, o. *Dyes*'. One modern editor reasonably translates this into the stage direction: 'He gives a long sigh and dies'. Actors often accompany and punctuate their articulate utterance with sighs, cries, groans, and moans, whether they are licensed by the text or not. The critic George Steiner shares a wonderfully vivid memory of the actress Helene Weigel playing the scene in Brecht's *Mother Courage and Her Children*, when soldiers try to force Courage to identify the body of her dead son. Twice she refuses. And then:

> As the body was carried off, Weigel looked the other way and tore her mouth wide open . . . . The sound that came out was raw and terrible beyond any description I could give of it. But in fact there was no sound. Nothing. The sound was total silence. It was silence which screamed and screamed through the whole theatre so that the audience lowered its head as before a gust of wind.

For better or worse, dramatists will always be at the mercy of performers (and directors), but good dramatists take care over the sounds they want us to hear. These include such signal stage effects as the famous knocking on the gate in *Macbeth* (a play particularly rich in its attention to sounds); the pistol shot at the end of Ibsen's *Hedda Gabler*; the breaking string at the end of Chekhov's *The Cherry Orchard*; the 'clearly audible rhythmic tread' specified for Beckett's *Footfalls* (1976); and the booming door that stars in Sam Shepard's *Fool for Love* (1983). They include the music that was integral to the performance of Greek choral lyrics (which were danced as well as sung); the trumpets and drums that call Shakespeare's men to war and the gentler strings that nurse Lear back from the grave; the tolling of the church bells that opens Lorca's *The House of Bernarda Alba*; the Schubert string quartet that gives Ariel Dorfman the title for *Death and the Maiden* (1991). The importance of sound to the cinema goes without saying.

But where tragedy is concerned, there is a scale by which sound is measured. It depends on the ancient but persistent sense of the place of human being between the gods and the beasts – not simply between but partly sharing the nature of both. As we look up, we imagine conversing with the tongues of angels, the flights of angels that Horatio prays will sing Hamlet to his rest. Whatever their religious beliefs, the great protagonists in Greek tragedy, in Marlowe, Shakespeare, and Racine, all strive to soar on the wings of their words, high above others, above origins, baseness, mindlessness. Tragedy honours these high aspirations, but it also punishes them.

The scream of agony reduces us to the level of the beasts – the animal of which Marsyas is half (but only half) composed. This is why the wordless exclamations of pain wrought into the very texture of tragedy are important. Translators struggle to find equivalents for the howls that erupt from the throats of Cassandra, Heracles, Oedipus, Philoctetes – exclamations which in transliteration sound like this: *aiai, oimoi, otototototoi popoi dā*, and *apappapai, papā papā papā papai*. Yet these are not simply animal sounds; they find their place in a line of verse. Shakespeare has less to play with, 'alack', 'alas', and 'woe', as well of course as 'O(h)' and 'Ah' (there are only 187 of the latter, but there are, bless the concordance, no fewer than 2,434 instances of the exclamatory 'O'). But he too puts them to work, and on the less formalized stages for which he wrote, the actor can take greater liberties with them and through them.

Nevertheless, the point about formality is crucial, or *has been* crucial to the idea of tragedy as a specific form of poetic drama. This idea was challenged in the 19th century by the descent of serious drama to the informality of prose and the dispersal of tragedy as a practice into other forms and media. Amongst contemporary practitioners, Tony Harrison raises a comparatively isolated voice in favour of the formality of verse. Think of the ancient Greek mask, he urges. During rehearsals of his version of the *Oresteia* he wrote to the director Peter Hall:

> Regular rhythm, form in poetry is like the mask it enables you to go beyond the scream as a reaction to events that in the normal course of life would make you do just that.

Beyond the scream, that is the challenge: not just to voice the agony of the victims, but to create the mask of art through which they speak and through which in turn they are viewed and heard.

The tragic scream is compounded of grief and of anger. In 1834 the 21-year-old Georg Büchner told his fiancée that he had been studying the history of the French Revolution: 'I felt shattered by the terrible fatalism of history.' Near the end of the play he went on to write, *Danton's Death*, Lucile Desmoulins mourns the husband who has just gone to the guillotine: 'Everything has the right to live. That gnat. That bird. So why not him?' There are echoes in this of Lear over Cordelia's corpse. Lucile feels the same horror as the protagonist of Büchner's other great play, *Woyzeck*. Life goes relentlessly on, an endless dance of death. Perhaps if she screamed loud enough, she could make it stop. Lucile sits down, covers her eyes, and screams. But it doesn't.

A century later, Brecht's Mother Courage waits to make a complaint outside an officer's tent during the Thirty Years' War. A young soldier comes storming in, very angry. She tells him to save his voice before he gets hoarse: 'People what shouts like that can't keep it up for ever.' He says it's unfair and he won't stand for it. She replies: 'And you're right; but how long? How long you not standing for unfairness? One hour, two hours? . . . your anger has gone up in smoke already, it was just a short one and you needed a long one, but where you going to get it from?'

Like the verbal arts, the visual arts can bear witness to 'unspeakable' horror, as Francisco Goya proves in the extraordinary series of etchings entitled *The Disasters of War* (Figure 13). These were prompted by the atrocities committed during the occupation of Spain by Napoleon's troops, and they look many years ahead to the

13. **O horror, horror, horror**

work of the photojournalists of our own times who have seized images of pain out of violent chaos (see Figure 17). Whatever the media it employs, the art of tragedy speaks for the stammerers, the dumb, the hoarse, the silenced, the dead.

Chapter 8
Timing

Acting

Tragedies are always concerned with the mysteries of timing, both good and bad, with the difficulty of knowing the right time to act or refrain from acting. 'To every thing there is a season, and a time to every purpose under the heaven. A time to be born, and a time to die; . . . A time to kill, and a time to heal; . . . ' (*Ecclesiastes*, 3, 1–3). These are beautiful and soothing truths to contemplate; but they are not always what you need when you've got something to *do*, as Hamlet and Orestes have. They are the generalizations in which Hamlet bathes as he steels himself for action, or flinches from it, we can't be certain which and neither can he. Tragedies tempt people to generalize. We want to be lifted up and out of time, as Chaucer lifts Troilus. We want to escape the pain of the here and now we've become embroiled with, whether as actors or spectators, the ordeal of *this* birth and *this* death, its unrepeatability.

'It's all in the timing.' The comedian needs it, but so does the athlete, the magician, the politician, the pilot, the lover, the assassin – everyone who has to 'act' or 'perform'. But these are tricky words. We use them for something that is really done or done for real, an action carried out and not just intended, pretended, or faked. What is done is done and cannot be undone, as the Macbeths discover. But to confuse matters, we also use the words 'act' and 'perform' in the opposite sense to mean something that is *not* done for real: imitation, fiction, play.

This doubleness is essential to all art that aspires to realism. Like the art of the Player King that so impresses Hamlet with 'Tears in his eyes, distraction in 's aspect' (II. ii. 556), or the art of the player who makes Hamlet's own passions and thoughts credible to us, or the art of the dramatist who creates them both. There's a particular challenge for all those involved in tragedy both on stage and off: they must get their timing right for the acts that go most badly wrong. It means that we can admire the actor's good timing even as we weep for the untimely death he or she is portraying. The more formalized the art, the more evident this will be. But it is a doubleness integral to all tragic art, the creation of a rhythm the spectator or reader is invited to share as the story moves to its climax.

This is no less true of opera or song, through which the affective power of music binds listener and performer more closely together than the spoken word or the visual image. Hence the special impact of the most dramatic singers, such as Maria Callas, not always by any means the most 'beautiful'. They draw the listener through time to their seemingly inevitable ending. Handel has a tragic cantata *Lucrezia* (1709), which you can hear performed in fine recordings in quite different styles by Janet Baker (Philips, 1972) and Magdalena Kožená (Archiv, 2000). The tragic effect depends on the way the singers lead us through the injured woman's contrasting passions up to the magnificent climax when she vows vengeance on the man who has raped her. She will be waiting for Tarquin in the underworld: *e furibonda e cruda nell'inferno / far ó far ó la mia vendetta* ('furious and savage, I shall have my revenge in hell').

What do we mean by a 'tragic act'? It is not an isolated event, any more than Lucrece is an isolated victim. It is part of a process of cause and effect. Tragedy brings together the figure who acts and the figure who suffers, Tarquin and Lucrece, the ones who do and the ones who are done to, as in Titian's painting of Apollo and Marsyas. (He also painted Tarquin and Lucrece several times.) Of course, the visual arts can also separate them. They can show us the gods who strike and will never be struck in return: look at 'The Striding God of Artemisium' (Figure 14). They can show us the victims on the receiving end, like the great embodiment of endurance by Ernst Barlach (Figure 15), which takes its title from the Nazi persecution of 'degenerate art' – *The Terrible Year* (1937). But the art of tragedy is to find or create the terrible moments they come together, the striker and the stricken, the action and passion, when someone is marked for life, if not doomed to death.

Two kinds of time

We do and are done to, endlessly, neither pure agents nor victims. We live in the active and passive 'voice', to use the grammatical term. There are other kinds of doubleness to the ways we live in time, in several tenses and moods all at once, in our sense of what was and will be, what should be and might have been, as well as what is. There is the difference we learn to live with between the knowledge that I am going to come to an end while life, the story, goes on. There is the exemplary case of Sophocles' Oedipus, the man who does not know what he's done, and then when he does, must face a new ignorance of his own future.

We can see the two aspects of time most important to tragedy in the sibling figures Orestes and Electra. For all the many differences in the ways their story is told by the three Greek tragedians (Aeschylus in *Libation Bearers*, Sophocles in *Electra*, Euripides in *Electra* and *Orestes*), their roles are defined by the plot. She waits; he will act. Orestes is the son who must do the deed: he must kill his mother to avenge his father. Electra is the female child who sides with her father, anticipating the loyalty of the goddess Athene in the final play of the *Oresteia*. Unable to act for herself but loyally awaiting his return from exile, Electra offers her brother a vital solidarity. This is

14. The striker

exactly the support that Hamlet doesn't get from Ophelia. It is hard
to say whether this is a cause or consequence of Hamlet's being
more than a bit of an Electra himself – and less of an Orestes than
her brother Laertes.

It is the waiting that Electra embodies, the experience of delay, of
suspense, of the endless endurance of tomorrow and tomorrow
and tomorrow. From this perspective, Orestes' arrival will always

15. The stricken

seem late, or belated, or as we say 'at long last' – *chronios*, as
Euripides' chorus describe the day of his return (585). At the end
of his *Electra*, Orestes chants: 'My sister, I see you now after such a
long separation (*chroniān* again), yet I am robbed at once of your
love and must leave you and be left by you!' (1308–10). It is a
word that Euripides seems to have applied to *Dikā*, Justice, in a
fragment that has come down to us. It is the word that Philoctetes

addresses to Heracles when he appears at the end of Sophocles' play (1446).

There is a sense in which 'belatedness' is a necessary component of tragedy. Thomas Hardy thought of titling one of his novels: 'Too Late, Beloved!' Then he wisely changed his mind and called it *Tess of the D'Urbervilles* instead. But there are different kinds of belatedness and different ways of representing them. There is Sophocles' Oedipus, and his horrified recognition of the time-lapse between our actions and our understanding of them. There is, for all the sons and daughters that populate tragedy, the sense of trailing in the wake of the parent-figures with whom they will never catch up – and catch with their surcease success, as Macbeth puts it (I. vii. 3–4). Artists who suffer from a feeling of belatedness can incorporate the need to get even with their predecessors as a form of artistic revenge. There is something of this in Euripides, and a great deal in Seneca. Worse still, there is the sense of being just another item in an endless and meaningless succession (like Hardy's Tess). Or to take a less singular perspective, there is the consciousness of collective belatedness in the structures of belief and practice inherited from the past, and the stories once replete with meaning and value, that made up a world into which we laggards are now too late to find entry. It's as if there ticked away inside our heads the idea of a momentous punctuality to which we will never be equal, from which we will never be free.

There is a word in Greek that complements this idea of belatedness. The word is *kairios* (the adjective) and *kairos* (the noun), and it means the right time, or high time, the being there or doing it. (As in the current colloquialism: 'I'll be there for you.') To some extent, it answers to our idea of crisis (a word that comes from the Greek for 'judgement') or climax (which comes from the Greek for a 'ladder'). It also carries the idea of what is meant in Shakespeare by 'occasion' and 'opportunity' – and the need to seize it. Iago, for example, has a highly developed sense of what is *kairios*: 'Even now, now, very now, an old black ram / Is tupping your white ewe'

(*Othello*, I. i. 88–9). *Kairios*: 'very now'. It is the sense of good timing needed by the conspirator, the artist, the killer.

This is exactly what the Paedagogus (or Tutor) has instilled into the Sophoclean Orestes. *Electra* revolves around a stark contrast between two senses of time. There is time as crisis and opportunity, time that is decisively plotted. And there is time as sheer duration, tomorrow and tomorrow and tomorrow, mere infinite tick-tock. The first is associated with action, decision, and plot – with Orestes; the second with patience, suffering, and waiting – with Electra. Orestes and Electra are reunited, but their two kinds of time meet in grievous collision. When she recognizes her brother, the Sophoclean Electra is ecstatic with joy; she cannot contain herself. But this Orestes has been wonderfully well prepared for his task; he is almost too good to be true, the inhumanly perfect instrument of justice. Does this Orestes need an Electra? She has lived for this moment, and now she is just in the way, a liability. She makes sure that she gets in on the act, to cry at their mother's murder, 'Strike her again a second time!' (1415), and to cut the wretched Aegisthus short when he asks to be allowed one final word. But the distances that have separated brother and sister can never be closed. They have bitten too deep. The plot which Orestes brings to fruition, completion – the last word of the play – can never assuage the pain that Electra has lived through so long.

Between times

The gods and the beasts do not pause for thought. To translate thought or impulse or volition into act is something we rightly admire and aspire to. It's a virtue in the soldier, surgeon, and athlete, in men and women who live and work at the sharpest end of the physical world where hesitation may be a matter of life and death.

The mastery of force has always been essential to tragedy. For the Greeks, the possibilities of physical might were focused in the legendary figure of Heracles, who cleared the world of its direst threats, its monsters. The risk of this force turning against itself and running amok is the subject of the two tragedies centred on him, Sophocles' *Women of Trachis* and Euripides' *Heracles*. There was also the physical prowess of the Homeric heroes, though we should note that the single most important attribute of Achilles was not strength but speed. We should also note the importance of their weapons, the great bow and arrows that Heracles bequeaths as a gift to the archer Philoctetes, and the armour of Achilles awarded not to the man of physical might, Ajax, but to the man of wiles, Odysseus. There are choices involved in the use and abuse of physical force. This is why it is important that Heracles is complemented by the other great philanthropist, Prometheus. Together they make possible the origins of the civilized life that distinguish man from the beasts. Prometheus gives us a start because he can, as his name suggests, see ahead. Or as Hamlet will have it, he can see 'before and after' (IV. iv: add. passage J, 28).

In her essay on Homer, Simone Weil writes:

> The man who is the possessor of force seems to walk through a non-resistant element; in the human substance that surrounds him nothing has the power to interpose between the impulse and the act, the tiny interval that is reflection.

This precious 'interval' recurs in tragedy, though it is not always tiny. We meet it in Aeschylus when Orestes pauses in front of his mother and turns to ask Pylades what he must do. It is the moment to which Shakespeare's Brutus gives memorable expression, as he prepares himself for the historic act that will bring the Roman Republic to an end and give birth in due course to the Empire – the murder of Julius Caesar.

> Between the acting of a dreadful thing
> And the first motion, all the interim is
> Like a phantasma or a hideous dream.
>
> (*Julius Caesar*, II. i. 63–5)

This looks ahead to the hideous dreams endured by Hamlet as he waits for the right moment, whenever that would be, to fulfil the Ghost's mission. Not when Claudius is at his prayers, evidently. (Euripides' Orestes kills Aegisthus at just such a moment, in the middle of a sacrifice.) There is the interim before the acting of a dreadful thing, but there is also the interim after, as Oedipus and Macbeth discover, as does King Lear.

Rites of passage

We can relate the hesitation caused by the reflection that 'act' and 'understanding' never quite cohere to more general patterns of human behaviour. Tragedies focus not just on painful predicaments but on acts of transition for individuals and communities. Anthropology has taught us to think of them as 'rites of passage'. These play an essential role in traditional societies, governing and controlling key moments of change, both for the individual and the social group: the transition from childhood to adulthood, from virginity to marriage, from life to death, from sowing to reaping, from peace to war. In their purest form, we can distinguish three phases in a rite of passage: separation, transition, and incorporation. It is the middle or 'liminal' phase – the word comes from the Latin for 'threshold' – that is important for our purposes.

It is not hard to see the classic periods of tragic drama in 5th-century Athens and early modern England, Spain, and France representing the collective experience of great historical transitions. We could try applying this idea to cultural production in 19th- and 20th-century Europe and North America; to the Germany of Goethe, Schiller, and Kleist; the Ireland of Synge, Yeats, and O'Casey; to Lorca's Spain and O'Neill's America; and beyond drama, to the Russia of Tolstoy, Dostoevsky, Pasternak, and Solzhenitsyn. But from the second half of the 19th century onwards, we must allow for the increasing pace of translation, for the process of diffusion and circulation that has brought the plays of Ibsen and the films of Ingmar Bergman to international audiences, and the horrors of the news into everyone's living rooms. Now everything everywhere seems to be liminal. Perhaps it always was, and it's only the false clarity of retrospect that allows us to create the temporal structures of history.

Rites of passage that are of obvious importance to tragedy are those that involve dying, funerals, and mourning. Gail Holst-Warhaft notes the traditional association of women with lament and the power it confers. We find, she says, a revealing anxiety displayed in ancient Greece at the birth of the city-state. Laws were passed to curb excessive mourning for the dead and to channel this power into the new political discourses of the funeral oration and tragic drama. We can see a certain conflict or negotiation between rural, popular, folk tradition, and urban, public, official art. And these dealings, she proposes, were gendered.

> Tragedy is an art preoccupied with death. It is, at least in part, an appropriation of the traditional art of women and we sense in its language, its inscrutable echoes of music and dance, an older body of ritual, a sub-stratum which informs and at times intrudes itself into an urban, male art.

One might hesitate to extend this particular model beyond ancient Athens, but it is highly plausible that tragedy should be characterized by *some* such struggle for control between rival group interests.

The value in getting the performance right and the danger in it going wrong are the nub of the matter. This is true of all rites of passage, not least the passage of power from parent to child, and from one generation to the next. Shakespeare's history plays are of obvious relevance here, but we should also think of the 'prodigious birth of love' in *Romeo and Juliet* (I. v. 139), of the accession to manhood in *Hamlet*, of the relinquishing of power in *King Lear*, *The Tempest*, and Wagner's *Ring* cycle. In theory, there is no real story in a rite of passage: one birth is much like another, one sexual initiation, wedding, coronation, harvest festival, graduation, funeral. But this is to look with too Olympian an eye. These things can go wrong. And tragedy represents the moments when they do, when the rites of passage are challenged, thwarted, violated, aborted. As they are in the 'maimèd rites' that disfigure Ophelia's funeral (*Hamlet*, V. i. 214), in the clandestine weddings of Romeo and Juliet, and Othello and Desdemona, in the ruptured ceremony at the heart of Lorca's *Blood Weddings*. This line of thought could be extended to the less spectacular customs that bind us together and regulate our social conduct, as when we welcome strangers over the threshold and share food with them round the table: rites murderously violated by the Macbeths.

Crisis and story

The visual arts have a complex relation to tragedy, not least in the way they arrest moments of crisis in time. The theatre is a visual art and particular moments in performance lodge in the mind's eye, for ever: images that can't be forgotten, such as Hamlet with Yorick's skull and Lear's entrance with Cordelia dead in his arms. In fact, there's a vigorous trade between the visual images promoted by the text, their realization in performance, their life in the mind of the reader and spectator, and the independent new life with which they're endowed by painters and artists. The history of Western art has been massively enriched by the visualization of scenes and figures from Homer, Aeschylus, Shakespeare, Corneille, and Racine.

Paintings, sculptures, and photographs can still the images that narrative keeps in motion. They can lift figures and scenes out of time, as the statues in Figures 14 and 15 seem to, or portraits and photos of the now dead and gone. The narrative arts of drama, novel, and cinema can be drawn to this stillness, and choose to exploit the idea of it, as witness all the paintings 'in' novels, like Lily Briscoe's painting in Virginia Woolf's *To the Lighthouse*. But the visual arts can also engage with narrative, and in any case where tragedy is potentially involved, whether it be sculpture, painting, or photograph, the idea of 'the story' will be an urgent one. It will raise all sorts of questions about what happened before, what happened after, what happened next, what happened 'then'. The spectator's relationship to such questions can be a complicated one. Indeed, we should probably reserve the idea of tragedy *in* the visual arts for those works in which the spectator's position is most vividly divided between times, between knowing what 'must' happen next and identifying with the bewildered figures within the work of art for whom the story is not yet over. Seeing is believing, and to see for yourself the acting out of a story is to believe that you might not know it after all, might not know how it will end *this* time.

The tragic witness occupies two different moments, inside and outside the time-world created by the work of art itself. This is the condition of the audience watching *Oedipus Tyrannus* or *King Lear*. We view the spectacle with godlike indifference because we all know how the story 'must go': it's fated, it's written. But we also view the spectacle with human passion because we identify with the characters who are making the story happen 'very now' (as Iago puts it), and who might, just might, make it happen differently this time.

There is a particular interest for tragedy in images that absorb and retain the sense of crisis. They allude powerfully to their moment in a sequence of events when the outcome is uncertain and the meaning, explanation, or interpretation of the story is open and unsettled. Even, or especially, when we 'know the story', or think that we do. Take Medea, for example, in a fine painting by Eugène Delacroix (Figure 16). We know how the story goes, but must it? The painting recaptures the critical moment when things could still have been, still be in this present tense, otherwise: when Medea has not yet killed her children.

There is an advantage here to tales, myths, and legends that 'we all' know, as 5th-century Athenians knew the stories about

16. The moment before what's done is done

17. Images that cry out for words

Oedipus and Orestes, and 16th-century Europeans knew the Scriptures that made, for example, Pieter Brueghel's paintings of *The Suicide of Saul* (1562) and *The Massacre of the Innocents* (c. 1566) intelligible. Since the late 18th century Shakespeare himself has to some extent provided a common treasury of traditional stories and figures, not only for the anglophone world. Yet it has become increasingly difficult in the advanced Western world to use these three words together: 'common', 'traditional', and 'treasury'. This has had a massive impact on the concept of tragedy, an impact that can be understood as depletion but also as liberation.

The process can be traced back some two hundred years to the point in time when Théodore Géricault made a great tragic painting out of a contemporary event. *The Raft of the Medusa* (1819) requires explanation. We don't know beforehand the story about these shipwrecked survivors, but it makes us want to, need to.

And this is the case with the shocking images that assault us daily on screen and in print. The photographs of Don McCullin make us want to know what has just happened and will happen – *did* happen – next. Like the image of six young people, one with a machine gun and another with a mandolin, serenading a corpse in the middle of the street (Figure 17). Who are they? Where are they and when? What is the photographer doing there, and what will become of him? Such images demand the ballast of words, explanation, and story. We need someone to tell us that this is a Muslim ghetto of East Beirut called Quarantina in 1976, that the revellers are Christian Falangists and the dead girl a young Palestinian. Yet so far from allaying the shock, words can deepen and engrave it. The photographer writes of the moment he stumbled on this scene: 'My mind was seized by this picture of carnival rejoicing in the midst of carnage.' Should he risk his life one more time and raise his camera? Then the mandolin-player calls him over, 'Hey, Mistah! Mistah! Come take photo!' Shortly afterwards, he hears there's a death warrant out for him.

Chapter 9
Endings

Blind hopes

'She saw in it the beginning of the end'. From the 19th century onwards (though not before that), 'the beginning of the end' has been a familiar phrase. The 'she' in this case is Hardy's Tess Durbeyfield, the morning after her disastrous honeymoon night with Angel Clare (chapter 37). Yet the next words try to seize the thought back: 'the temporary end, at least, for the revelation of his tenderness by the incident of the night raised dreams of a possible future with him'. So hope is not dead for Tess; perhaps not *the* end just yet.

It is hard to be sure when an ending begins, though this does not stop us from trying. In Beckett's *Waiting for Godot*, Pozzo explodes: 'Have you not done tormenting me with your accursed time!' But calming down, he reflects: 'They give birth astride of a grave, the light gleams an instant, then it's night once more.' Beginning, middle, and end: this conforms impeccably to Aristotle's definition of an action. It has a pleasantly sedative effect, on the speaker at least, with its illusion of superiority to the here and now.

Ending is more than a moment in time. It takes and needs time, as the grammatical form of the word suggests. It is comforting to hear the bell for the last lap, to know that this is the fifth and final set, that there are three minutes of 'normal time' left. But unless we are terminally bored by the proceedings, we don't just need to know *that* it will end, we want to know *how*. When it's all over, can we look back and discern the moment when it all started to go wrong or come right, the moment when there was still hope, no hope, new hope, the moment when it all became clear? This pattern cannot be measured and defined in advance but only interpreted in retrospect, and that with no real certainty.

What if we *could* know the future, as Macbeth so desperately wants? Prometheus has saved the human race from Zeus' plan to obliterate it and create a new one, but when the chorus press him on what else he has done for humanity, he tells them that he stopped mortals from foreseeing their doom: 'I planted in them blind hopes' (250). Hope has to be blind. If we could see the future, then we might just sit down and despair. This is why it's so miserable to be Teiresias in *Oedipus Tyrannus*. Being blessed and cursed with inhuman foresight, Teiresias has no will to intervene in what he knows to be inevitable, while Oedipus, being cursed and blessed with human blindness, cannot escape the desire and need to take action. As readers and audience we are invited to share both Teiresias' helpless vision and Oedipus' striving blindness.

Tragedies raise painful questions about ends, endings, and dreams of a possible future, whether in this world or another. We do not know for certain how long we have got here. Modern genetics may tell us (and our insurance companies) more than we wish (them) to know about how long we are likely to have. But nothing can legislate against untimely accident, and there are no insuperable obstacles to making a premature end of ourselves. Tragedy makes a mockery of average life expectancy, as it does of average everything else. 'The readiness is all', so Hamlet stoically concludes (V. ii. 168). *All*? Like most leading characters in tragedy, Hamlet is too full of passion and energy and aspiration to be content just quietly to wait. Pascal famously remarks that all our misery derives from being unable to stay put, at rest, in a room. There is a lot of waiting in tragedy, but it is fraught with desire for someone to come or something to happen 'in time'.

Missing corpses

What does it mean for a tragedy to end well? Can tragedy do without at least one corpse and preferably several? We might think not, considering the end of Sophocles' *Antigone*, where Creon is surrounded by the dead on stage and off – Antigone, Polyneices, his son Haemon, and wife Eurydice – or the end of *Hamlet*, when the stage is littered with corpses; or the end of all the versions of the Phaedra-and-Hippolytus story by Euripides, Seneca, and Racine. There is a reasonable presumption that someone should do the decent thing and meet their end at the end of a tragedy, as Ibsen's Hedda Gabler does, and Commandant Frank Butler, Brian Friel's Theseus figure in *Living Quarters*.

On the other hand, one can readily think of plays that do not *end* with a corpse, though they may have been strewn along the way: the *Oresteia*, for instance. There is only one death in the course of Sophocles' *Ajax*, but it occurs half way through when the title character falls on his sword (or Hector's sword, to be precise); the rest of the play deals with the aftermath. Other significant characters die in the middle of plays, such as Mercutio in *Romeo and Juliet*; Julius Caesar in the play named after him; Duncan and Banquo and Macduff's family in *Macbeth*; or the Allmers' young child in Ibsen's most terrible play, *Little Eyolf*. In *Antony and Cleopatra*, Shakespeare carefully orchestrates the sequence of three deaths with which the play draws to its close: Enobarbus, Antony, Cleopatra. (There is no question which of the three is the most painful – the first.) Then there are the deaths that occur before the play begins and then loom over the action: Iphigeneia in *Agamemnon*, Polyneices in *Antigone*, old Hamlet, the father of young Titus in Racine's *Bérénice*, and the Kellers' boy Larry in Miller's *All My Sons*.

Most, though not all, of these deaths are 'untimely', in a sense comparable to the birth of the child in *Macbeth* who was ripped untimely from his mother's womb. Cleopatra's would be an exception, perhaps Antony's also. Death may be a timely deliverance, as it is for Sophocles' Oedipus when he reaches Colonus. Death would be a release for any number of characters in modern tragedies, like the trio who sit down together at the end of Chekhov's *Uncle Vanya* to face a future now robbed of all meaning, or the Tyrone family in O'Neill's *A Long Day's Journey into Night*. 'Now we are left in Hell', declares the villainous De Flores near the end of Middleton's *The Changeling*, moments before dying with his partner in crime, Beatrice-Joanna. 'We are all there, it circumscribes here', replies her shattered father, Vermandero.

Can you have tragedy with, as we say, a 'good outcome'? One way for a tragedy to end well, or even 'happily', would be for the threat of death to be averted, as it is at the end of the *Oresteia*, when Orestes is acquitted, or the end of Euripides' *Alcestis*, when the wife and mother is brought back from the dead and restored to her shameful husband, Admetus. There are other such plays of Euripides (including *Iphigeneia at Tauris*, *Helen*, *Ion*, and *Orestes*) that entail what has been called 'catastrophe survived'. They suggest the elasticity of genre for ancient Greek dramatists. But artists have always seen generic conventions as an opportunity to play with expectations rather than a set of rules to be followed.

There are other suggestive cases, such as the verse drama in which Goethe gave fullest expression to the Enlightenment's vision of Greece, his *Iphigenie auf Tauris* (1786–7). How far does the play endorse its heroine's belief in the possibility of universal reconciliation? There is no critical consensus. No less troublesome is the series of plays produced by Pierre Corneille between 1640 and 1642, from *Horace* through *Cinna* to *Polyeucte*. They can be read as a sequence of inquiries into the possibility of good or even ideal government. There is a sense in which all three end 'well'. (Also *Le*

Cid (1637), which can be seen as a kind of prologue.) In *Horace* the eponymous hero is put on trial for killing his sister Camille on his return from the battlefield, where he has saved Rome by slaying all three of the enemy champions. One of them is betrothed to Camille. In the great scene of confrontation between triumphant brother and distraught sister, she denounces his *brutalité* and rails blasphemously against Rome. His patience snaps and he runs her through. Though he says himself that he is content to die – *La mort seule aujourd'hui peut conserver ma gloire* (V. ii. 1580, 'only death today can save my name and fame') – and though the King describes the killing as *énorme*, the judgement goes in his favour and he is spared. The state needs the martial force that Horace represents, just as Duncan cannot do without Macbeth (nor Malcolm without Macduff). If it weren't for Horace, Rome would now be enslaved. The King's clinching line is this: *Ta vertu met ta gloire au-dessus de ton crime* (V. iii. 1760, 'Your "virtue" puts your "renown" above your crime'). Whatever *vertu* and *gloire* mean here – whatever the King wants them to mean – they are more important than Horace's crime.

Cinna continues this line of thought. In the final scene, the emperor Auguste breaks not only with ordinary justice but conventional notions of political expedience. (It was Napoleon's favourite play.) Again, he acts in the interests of the state when he pardons the man on trial, the conspirator Cinna, traitor to the state. But in so far as Cinna is the equivalent not of the 'loyal' Horace but the 'treacherous' Camille, Auguste's mercy is now on a higher ethical level than his predecessor's in *Horace*. The eponymous hero of *Polyeucte* takes the issues to a more elevated plane again. He is a traitor both to the Roman state and to his own family: a partisan convert to Christianity, his allegiance is to God. In insisting on his own martyrdom, he seeks not to save the state (like Horace) nor to ensure its future security (like Auguste), but to start the revolution that will found a new polity on the ruins of the old. His death makes immediate converts of his wife and her father. The days of the pagan Empire are numbered.

Along with the *Oresteia*, *Philoctetes*, *Alcestis*, and others, these plays of Corneille make us reflect that in any process involving great pain and risk to all involved, a 'good outcome' may not obliterate the trauma that precedes it. It provides no guarantee against relapse nor immunity against new traumas. Corneille also prompts questions about whether the outcome really *is* good. Good for whom? Horace is silent in the face of the King's judgement. Perhaps he would have preferred to die. There are other figures alive and dead, including Camille, whose voices are overridden in the officially approved conclusion. Auguste establishes a reign of peace, but can he forget the blood he has shed on his route to the absolute power that he now enjoys? His final words – and the final words of the play – are *tout oublier* (V. iii. 1780, 'forget everything'). Can he? Should he? Can the blood already shed be entirely erased from the record, this side of paradise? These tragedies suggest that no outcome can be so purely good that we should forget the reality of the pain suffered and the cost incurred in reaching it.

Promiscuous events

The critic John Dennis had few doubts about what it should mean for a tragedy to end well. In 1712 he complained of Shakespeare's tragedies, that:

> the good and the bad perishing promiscuously ... , there can be none or very weak instruction in them: for such promiscuous events call the government of providence into question, and by skeptics and libertines are resolved into chance.

Dennis is promoting what we call 'poetical justice' and the genre that depends on it, where virtue is rewarded and vice is punished. Melodrama gives us a view of the world that confirms who are the good guys and who are the bad. It denies the operations of chance and resists the chaos of promiscuity. Dennis is right, not just about Shakespeare, that tragedies do call government into question. Plato would have applauded his protest; so would most political leaders, now as always. And Samuel Johnson concurred when he remarked, apropos the death of Cordelia, that 'since all reasonable beings naturally love justice, I cannot easily be persuaded, that the observation of justice makes a play worse.' No wonder Nahum Tate's version of *King Lear* held the English stage for so long with its happy ending, Cordelia living and married to Edgar.

The endings of tragedies call much into question, not least the matter of who and what is rightly to be judged 'good' and 'bad'. Death is promiscuous in tragedy. It engulfs the good, the bad, and the indifferent without regard to their moral qualities, the Cordelias as well as the Gonerils and Regans. There is no justice we can recognize in the way war, famine, and plague choose their victims. That's what happens with the weapons of mass destruction – they do not discriminate. The 'evil' that tragedy shows us is a realistic assessment of the way individuals are destroyed with no regard to whether they deserve it or not. This is why Dennis's formula is hopelessly inadequate to the instruction that tragedy really does afford. It gives us a vision of chaos: '*c'est là où règnent le désordre et l'inquiétude*', writes the Abbé d'Aubignac in 1657: tragedy is 'the place ruled by disorder and anxiety'. Tragedy does offer instruction, and *pace* Dennis, it is not weak. Traditional humanist accounts from Hegel to A. C. Bradley and their heirs take pride in the heroic virtues embodied in an Oedipus, an Antigone, a Lear, a Cordelia. But perhaps what we should look for in tragedy is instruction in humility.

This is one aspect of tragedy: the cruel, anarchic element that Nietzsche rejoiced in. Tragedy revels in exposing the poverty of the ethical categories that a Dennis tries to take his stand on. As if it were meaningful to ponder whether Hamlet or Lear or Oedipus or Antigone or Medea were or were not 'good'. But this is not the whole truth. At the end of *Bacchae* it is hard to share Dionysus' indifference to the carnage he has wrought. It is more natural to protest with Cadmus that the gods *ought* to be better than this, better than *us*. At the end of Seneca's *Thyestes* and *Medea*, it is difficult to feel jubilation at the cosmic void. Thyestes prays that the gods will punish Atreus, the brother who has killed his children and made him unwittingly eat them. But it is Atreus who has the last word: *Te puniendum liberis trado tuis* ('To thy sons for punishment do I deliver thee'). There is no sign that the gods have heard Thyestes, nor that they even exist. Plenty of punishment, but where's the justice? Strindberg urges us to take 'uninhibited pleasure' in the destruction of his superannuated aristocrat, Miss Julie: 'a relief such as one feels when one sees an incurable invalid at last allowed to die'. Can we? Do we share Maxim Gorky's glee at the demolition of the Ranevskaya family in Chekhov's *Cherry Orchard*: 'egotistical like children, with the flabbiness of senility. They missed the right moment for dying'?

It is tempting to simplify, as Dennis wished that Shakespeare had, to distinguish the sheep from the goats, the victims from the punishers, and administer justice to both – if it is indeed justice. But tragedians refuse to cooperate. *Punishment Without Revenge* (1634) is the deceptively blithe title of one of Lope de Vega's most disturbing plays. It would take a peculiarly ruthless viewer or reader to concur with the justice done by the lascivious Duke on the wife and (illegitimate) son he has driven into each other's arms (a powerful variation on the Phaedra myth). Like other ministers of justice, such as Kyd's Hieronymo in *The Spanish Tragedy* and Vindice in *The Revenger's Tragedy*, Lope's Duke of Ferrara gets caught up – along with his victims – in a lethal process that wreaks havoc with the simple categories of 'good' and 'bad'.

Resolution

We take it for granted that conflict is at the heart of tragedy. For this we mainly have Hegel to thank. Less easy to accept are his arguments about the role of 'resolution' and 'reconciliation' in tragedy. These may well be 'fully comprehensible only against the backdrop of Hegel's larger conception of history as the violent self-embodiment of Spirit (*Geist*) in space and time'. But if we don't share Hegel's conception of history, this is not going to be much help when it comes to the death of Cordelia.

The author of *Shakespearean Tragedy* (1904) was one of the most influential agents for the domestication in English of Hegelian ideas. A. C. Bradley writes with care about the 'bewilderment', 'dismay', and 'protest' caused by Cordelia's death. But precisely because the ending arouses these feelings so powerfully in us, it provokes, he suggests, a countervailing sense of acceptance and 'reconciliation'. Why? Because it gives us the impression that the heroic being is 'superior to the world' and is 'rather set free from life than deprived of it'. Cordelia's unjust and untimely death *proves* the superiority of another realm of transcendent value. She is, one might say, too good to live. This is a prime example of what philosophical spectators can make of tragedy when they stand well back from the shock of it. Bradley even reproves Hegel for failing to recognize that in some tragedies – *Hamlet*, *Othello*, *King Lear* – 'pain is mingled not merely with acquiescence, but with something like exultation'. This would have bewildered and dismayed Dr Johnson.

Bradley's focus is on what he calls 'our feeling at the close of the conflict' (378). In other words, the 'reconciliation' he urgently seeks is something that happens in us, the readers and viewers. This takes us back to the questions raised by the notion of *katharsis*. Where does it – whatever it is – take place? On stage or in the audience? There are instances in which 'reconciliation' happens *within* the dramatic action, most notably in the massive resolution of conflicting claims at the close of the *Oresteia*. Yet most tragedies that seem good examples of the genre, including Hegel's own favourite, *Antigone*, come nowhere near the display of such final concord. It is true that we find many instances in tragedy of personal reconciliation between estranged individuals, as, for example, between Lear and Cordelia, or Coriolanus and his mother Volumnia, or indeed Theseus and his dying son Hippolytus. But the relation of these particular reunions to the total action is tricky, and their effect on our sense of the conclusion as a whole elusive.

It may help to think a bit harder about the words we use in this context and the ideas they entail: 'resolution', 'reconciliation' – and now, for better or worse, the ubiquitous 'closure'. On 3 November 1979 in Greensboro, North Carolina, five people were killed by members of the Ku Klux Klan and American Nazi Party during a march for racial, social, and economic justice. Nearly 25 years later, Greensboro announced a Truth and Reconciliation Commission, the first of its kind in the United States, an 'historic effort to honestly confront its tragedy of November 3, 1979 . . . . The passage of time alone cannot bring closure.' The last 30 years have seen the proliferation of Truth Commissions set up to investigate human rights abuses, including war crimes. Many associate 'Truth' with the word 'Reconciliation' – in Chile (1990), South Africa (1995), Sierra Leone (1999), and East Timor (2001), for example. Common to these projects is an idea of 'restorative justice' that seeks to differentiate itself from traditional retributive justice in the cause of reparation, forgiveness, and healing.

The arts of tragedy are much concerned with the difficulties and possibilities of justice, truth, and reconciliation. They return no simple answers. We might more fully appreciate the complexity with which great tragedies end by reflecting further on 'resolution' and 'resolve', words with a wider range of meanings than 'reconciliation' and 'reconcile'. We think of the resolution of a problem, of the resolution with which we *meet* a problem, of the resolution formally agreed by an assembly or meeting. There are more technical senses of the word, in optics and music for example, and older meanings now rare or obsolete, in physiology and mathematical logic. But from Shakespeare's time onwards, the dominant senses of 'resolution' have linked the idea of an ending to qualities of strength, determination, and courage required to bring it about. 'And let us swear our resolution', Casca exhorts his fellow-conspirators (*Julius Caesar*, II. i. 113); 'We have no

friend / But resolution, and the briefest end', declares Cleopatra
(*Antony and Cleopatra*, IV. xvi. 92–3); 'To be once in doubt is
once to be resolv'd', so Othello believes (III. iii. 183–4),
epitomizing the decisiveness that Hamlet lacks, for better and
worse, the Hamlet who finds 'the native hue of resolution . . .
sicklied o'er with the pale cast of thought' (III. i. 86–7).

But it is also Hamlet who reminds us in his first soliloquy of the
Latin roots of the word:

> O that this too too solid flesh would melt,
> Thaw, and resolve itself into a dew, . . .

(I. ii.129–30)

Here 'resolve' is virtually equivalent to our 'dissolve'. Hamlet is close
to the sense in which St Paul uses the noun when he tells Timothy
that 'The tyme of my resolucion or deeth, is ny'. This is Wyclif
translating the Vulgate's *resolutio* in 1382; two hundred years later
the Rheims New Testament follows suit (but the King James
version has 'departure'). 'Resolutio' is itself a translation of the
Greek New Testament's *analysis*, a word well known to Sophocles,
whose chorus see no prospect of 'release' for Electra from her
miseries (142). Seen from this aspect, *analysis* or resolution is
something of which you are the object, something that happens to
you, a loosening of yourself, your body, your identity, whether this is
conceived as deliverance or destruction, whether it inspires desire
or dread. Tragedy stages both the desire and dread inspired by the
prospect of our own resolution into dust, into thin air, into other
forms of being.

Hamlet speaks of the flesh resolving itself as if it were a process in
which he could take or wished to take no part. Tragedies happen.
But tragedies are also made, and the art of tragedy insists that we
grasp this paradox. There are all kinds of resolution in which we
could or should play an active role. We can subject other things to
the process of resolution and see more clearly the elements of which

they are composed. This is what the word meant to Aristotle, the 'resolution of a problem by the analysis of its conditions', the opposite of *synthesis*. Tragedy is in this sense an art of analysis.

Release, dispersal, destruction, but also clarity, understanding, revelation: all these ideas are pregnant in the 'resolution' that reaches us from Latin. All are essential to the reverberations with which great tragedies continue to end.

References

All references in the text to Homer, Aeschylus, Sophocles,
Euripides, Seneca, and Virgil are to the Loeb Classical Library
editions (Cambridge, Mass., and London), from which translations
are also taken (figures in parentheses are line numbers): Homer,
Iliad, 2 vols, tr. A. T. Murray, revised by William F. Wyatt (1999);
Aeschylus, 2 vols, tr. Herbert Weir Smyth (1922, 1926; reprinted
with appendix by Hugh Lloyd-Jones, 1963); Sophocles, 3 vols, ed.
and tr. Hugh Lloyd-Jones (1994–6); Euripides, 6 vols, ed. and tr.
David Kovacs (1994–2002); Seneca, *Tragedies I*, ed. and tr. John
G. Fitch (2002), and *Tragedies II*, tr. Frank Justus Miller (1917);
Virgil, *Eclogues, Georgics, Aeneid I–VI*, tr. H. Rushton Fairclough,
revised by G. P. Goold (1999). All Greek words have been
transliterated. References to Shakespeare are to *The Complete
Works*, general eds Stanley Wells and Gary Taylor (Oxford, 1986:
references to *King Lear* are to the text printed as *The Tragedy of
King Lear*); Corneille to *Théâtre complet*, 3 vols, eds Georges
Couton (vol. 1) and Maurice Rat (vols 2, 3), Classiques Garnier
(Paris, 1971–4), and Racine to *Théâtre complet*, eds Jacques Morel
and Alain Viala, Classiques Garnier (Paris, 1980): translations are
my own. References to the Old and New Testaments are to the
Oxford World's Classics edition of the King James version of *The
Bible* (Oxford, 1998). Given the variety of easily available editions in
which well known novels by George Eliot and Thomas Hardy can
be read, I have in such cases supplied references to chapters only.

Chapter 1

Milton, 'Sometime let gorgeous Tragedy': 'Il Penseroso' (1645), *Complete Shorter Poems*, ed. John Carey (London, 1971), p. 143; 'the small esteem or rather infamy': 'Of That Sort of Dramatic Poem Which Is Called Tragedy', introduction to *Samson Agonistes* (1670), *Complete Shorter Poems*, p. 342. Sir Philip Sidney, *A Defence of Poetry* (1595), in Brian Vickers, *English Renaissance Literary Criticism* (Oxford, 1999), p. 383. Francesco da Buti and Giovanni da Serravalle quoted by Henry Ansgar Kelly, *Ideas and Forms of Tragedy from Aristotle to the Middle Ages* (Cambridge, 1993), pp. 156, 207. 'Emotions most likely to be stirred': Aristotle, *Poetics*, tr. M. E. Hubbard, *Ancient Literary Criticism*, eds D. A. Russell and M. Winterbottom (Oxford, 1972), p. 103. Brueghel's 'Icarus': W. H. Auden, 'Musée des Beaux Arts', *Collected Poems*, ed. Edward Mendelson (London 1976; revised edn 1991), p. 179. 'Real-life' tragedy from Nero to Thomas Walsingham: Kelly, *Ideas and Forms of Tragedy*, pp. 22–4, 91–2, 170. Artaud quoted by Martin Esslin, *Artaud*, Fontana Modern Masters (London, 1976), p. 11. Chaucer, *The Canterbury Tales*, *Works*, ed. F. N. Robinson, 2nd edn (London, 1957), p. 189. 'Poetry speaks more of universals': *Poetics*, tr. Stephen Halliwell (London, 1987), p. 41; 'poetry tends to make general statements': *Poetics*, tr. Hubbard, *Ancient Literary Criticism*, p. 102. 'Medicine must drown threnodies': Plato, *Republic*, Book 10, tr. D. A. Russell, *Ancient Literary Criticism*, p. 72. Jonas Barish, *The Anti-Theatrical Prejudice* (Berkeley and London, 1981). 'Through the arousal of pity and fear': *Poetics*, tr. Halliwell, p. 37. 'One recent critic': A. D. Nuttall, *Why Does Tragedy Give Pleasure?* (Oxford, 1996), p. 6. 'The impulse to approach': I. A. Richards, *Principles of Literary Criticism* (London, 1924; reprinted 1967), p. 193. 'Compassionate grief': W. B. Stanford, *Greek Tragedy and the Emotions* (London, 1983), pp. 23–4.

Chapter 2

George Steiner, *The Death of Tragedy* (London, 1961), pp. 114, 320. W. H. Auden, 'Writing', *The Dyer's Hand* (London, 1963), p. 25.

Chaplin, in A. Norman Jeffares and Martin Gray (eds), *Collins Dictionary of Quotations* (Glasgow, 1995), p. 152. Lucien Goldmann, *Racine*, tr. Alastair Hamilton (Cambridge, 1972), p. 7. Vase paintings of the murder of Agamemnon: H. A. Shapiro, *Myth into Art: Poet and Painter in Classical Greece* (London and New York, 1994), pp. 125–30. Re-writing the Greeks: see, for example, Seneca's *Phaedra*, *Medea*, and *Hercules Furens* (middle of the 1st century AD), Racine's *Andromaque* (1667), *Iphigénie* (1674), and *Phèdre* (1677), Gluck's operas *Alceste* (1767), *Iphigénie en Aulide* (1774), and *Iphigénie en Tauride* (1779). I. A. Richards, *Principles of Literary Criticism* (London, 1924; reprinted 1967), p. 194. Peri's *Euridice* quoted by Tim Carter, 'The Seventeenth Century', in Roger Parker (ed.), *The Oxford Illustrated History of Opera* (Oxford, 1994), p. 11. *The Death of Klinghoffer*, see *www.usopera.com/operas/deathofk.html*, and the film version directed by Penny Woolcock for Channel 4. Hegel and the language of poetry: *Hegel on Tragedy*, eds Anne and Henry Paolucci (New York, 1962), p. 31. Steiner on Claudel, *Death of Tragedy*, pp. 333–41. Modern versions of Greek tragedy: Ezra Pound, Sophocles' *Women of Trachis* (1956) and (with Rudd Fleming) *Elektra* (1990), Wole Soyinka, *The Bacchae* (1973), Tony Harrison, *Oresteia* (1981), Tom Paulin, *The Riot Act* (*Antigone*, 1985), Seamus Heaney, *The Cure at Troy* (*Philoctetes*, 1991), and *The Burial at Thebes* (*Antigone*, 2004), Timberlake Wertenbaker, *The Thebans* (1992), Derek Mahon, *The Bacchae* (1991), and Ted Hughes, *Oresteia* and *Alcestis* (both 1999). Ibsen on prose, letter to Edmund Gosse, 15 January 1874, reprinted in *Henrik Ibsen: A Critical Anthology*, ed. James McFarlane (Harmondsworth, 1970), p. 83. E. M. Forster, 'Ibsen the Romantic' (1928), reprinted in *Abinger Harvest* (1936). Lorca quoted by H. A. Ramsden in his edition of *La Casa de Bernarda Alba* (Manchester, 1983), p. xxix.

Chapter 3

'If way to the Better there be': 'In Tenebris II', *Complete Poetical Works of Thomas Hardy*, ed. Samuel Hynes, vol. 1 (Oxford, 1982),

p. 208. Ariel Dorfman, 'Afterword' to *Death and the Maiden* (London, 1991; revised edn 1994), pp. 49, 48. O'Neill, *Long Day's Journey into Night* (New Haven and London, 1955), p. 170. Oliver Sacks, *Awakenings* (1973; revised edn 1990), p. 55. 'She dwelt among the untrodden ways', *William Wordsworth: The Poems*, vol. I, ed. John O. Hayden (New Haven and London, 1977), p. 366. Brecht, *Life of Galileo*, tr. John Willett (London, 1980), pp. 110, 158. Miller, Introduction to *Collected Plays* (1957), *Theatre Essays*, 2nd edn, ed. Robert A. Martin (London, 1994), p. 170.

Chapter 4

'The first principle': *Poetics*, tr. Halliwell, p. 38; 'the figure who falls between these types', tr. Halliwell, p. 44. Miller, introduction to *Collected Plays*, *Theatre Essays*, p. 130. Corneille cited by John D. Lyons, *Kingdom of Disorder: The Theory of Tragedy in Classical France* (West Lafayette, Indiana, 1999), pp. 138–9. Freud, 'Psychopathic Characters on the Stage', tr. James Strachey, *Art and Literature*, ed. Albert Dickson, Penguin Freud Library, vol. 14 (Harmondsworth, 1985), pp. 119–28. Nietzsche, *The Genealogy of Morals*, Second Essay, III (1887), tr. Francis Golffing (with *The Birth of Tragedy*) (New York, 1956), p. 194. Schiller, *Mary Stuart*, tr. Hilary Collier Sy-Quia and Peter Oswald (with *Don Carlos*) (Oxford, 1996), Act IV, scenes xi–xii, Act V, scene xiv.

Chapter 5

F. W. H. Myers quoted by Gordon Haight, *George Eliot: A Biography* (Oxford, 1968), p. 464. President Wilson, *The Penguin Book of Twentieth-Century Speeches*, ed. Brian Macarthur (Harmondsworth, 2000), p. 61. George Eliot, 'The *Antigone* and Its Moral', *Selected Essays, Poems and Other Writings*, eds A. S. Byatt and Nicholas Warren (Harmondsworth, 1990), pp. 363–6. Margaret Olivia Little, 'Moral Generalities Revisited', *Moral Particularism*, eds Brad Hooker and Margaret Olivia Little (Oxford, 2000), p. 304. Raymond Williams, *Modern Tragedy* (London, 1966; revised edn 1979), and Terry Eagleton, *Sweet*

Violence: The Idea of the Tragic (Oxford, 2003). Adorno, *Aesthetic Theory*, tr. C. Lenhardt (London, 1984), p. 42. Barthes quoted by Alain Robbe-Grillet as the epigraph to 'Nature, Humanism and Tragedy' (1958), *Snapshots and Towards a New Novel*, tr. Barbara Wright (London, 1965), p. 75; 'Tragedy is only a way', p. 95. Nuttall, *Why Does Tragedy Give Pleasure?*, p. 75. Nietzsche, '[T]he metaphysical solace': *The Birth of Tragedy*, tr. Francis Golffing (New York, 1956), p. 50. Yeats, 'The Tragic Theatre' (1910), reprinted in *Essays and Introductions* (London, 1961), p. 240. Nietzsche, 'How much blood and horror': *Genealogy of Morals*, tr. Golffing, p. 194. Walter Benjamin, *Illuminations*, ed. Hannah Arendt, tr. Harry Zohn (London, 1970), p. 258. William James, *The Principles of Psychology* (1890), cited by Richard Poirier, 'In Praise of Vagueness: Henry and William James', *Trying It Out in America: Literary and Other Performances* (New York, 1999), p. 240. Pound, *Sophocles, Women of Trachis* (London, 1969), p. 66.

Chapter 6

Chaucer, *Troilus and Criseyde*, *Works*, ed. F. N. Robinson, 2nd edn (London, 1957), p. 479. Lawrence, Preface to *Touch and Go: A Play in Three Acts* (1920), p. 9. Angela Carter, *Wise Children* (London, 1991), p. 213. Mel Brooks, cited as epigraph to Gary Larson, *The Prehistory of the Far Side* (1990). Wilde quoted by Richard Ellmann, *Oscar Wilde* (London, 1987), p. 441. Bergson, *Le Rire* (1900), tr. Cloudesley Brereton and Fred Rothwell as *Laughter: An Essay on the Meaning of the Comic* (London, 1911), p. 5. 'Desdemona was put to bed', quoted by Julie Hankey, introduction to *Othello*, Plays in Performance (Bristol, 1987), p. 77. Lehrer, first recorded in *An Evening Wasted with Tom Lehrer* (1959) and frequently re-released. Baudelaire, 'Of the Essence of Laughter, and generally of the Comic in the Plastic Arts' (1855), *Baudelaire: Selected Writings on Art and Artists*, tr. P. E. Charvet (Harmondsworth, 1972), pp. 140–61. Plato, *Republic*, Book 10, tr. Russell, *Ancient Literary Criticism*, p. 72. Auden, 'Writing', *The Dyer's Hand*, p. 25. Marx, *The Eighteenth Brumaire of Louis*

Bonaparte (1852), extracts in *Karl Marx: A Reader*, ed. Jon Elster (Cambridge, 1986), p. 276. Chekhov's Vershinin, *Three Sisters* [with *Ivanov* and *The Seagull*], tr. Ronald Hingley (London, 1968), p. 135. Bergson, 'A laughable expression': *Laughter*, p. 24; 'But a comic expression': *Laughter*, p. 25. T. S. Eliot, *Complete Plays and Poems* (London, 1969), p. 25. Chekhov, *The Note-Books of Anton Chekhov*, tr. S. S. Koteliansky and Leonard Woolf (London, 1921), p. 77. Camus, *The Myth of Sisyphus*, tr. Justin O'Brien (Harmondsworth, 1975), p. 109.

Chapter 7

Tragedy

George Eliot, Introduction to *Felix Holt* (1866). Weil, 'Human Personality', *Simone Weil: An Anthology*, ed. Sian Miles (London, 1986), p. 72. Tony Harrison, *Selected Poems*, 2nd edn (London, 1987), p. 121; 'an avenger speaking for the silent': Blake Morrison, 'The Filial Art', *Tony Harrison*, Bloodaxe Critical Anthologies, ed. Neil Astley (Newcastle upon Tyne, 1991), p. 54. John Ford, *The Broken Heart*, ed. T. J. B. Spencer, Revels Plays (Manchester, 1980), V. iii. pp. 75-6. T. S. Eliot, 'What is a Classic?' (1944), *On Poetry and Poets* (London, 1957), p. 62. Christ before Pilate, *Gospels according to St Matthew*, 27, 12—14, and *St Mark* 15, 3-5. Beckett's *Not I*, *Collected Shorter Plays* (London, 1984), pp. 213-23. Harrison on 'poetry after Auschwitz': 'Facing up to the Muses' (1988), Bloodaxe Anthology, pp. 429-54. Steiner on Helene Weigel's Mother Courage, *The Death of Tragedy*, pp. 353-4. O'Neill, *Long Day's Journey*, p. 154. Lorca, *Deep Song and Other Prose*, ed. and tr. Christopher Maurer (London and Boston, 1980), p. 25. Harrison, 'The School of Eloquence', *Selected Poems*, pp. 111, 112. One modern editor of *Hamlet*: G. R. Hibbard (Oxford, 1987), p. 352. 'Regular rhythm, form in poetry': Harrison, Bloodaxe Anthology, p. 280. 'I felt shattered': Büchner, *Complete Plays*, ed. Michael Patterson (London, 1987), p. 290; Lucile's scream, p. 79. Brecht, *Mother Courage and her Children*, tr. John Willett (London and New York, 1980), pp. 44-5.

Chapter 8

Euripides, Fragment 223, *Tragicorum Graecorum Fragmenta*, ed. August Nauck , 2nd edn (Lipsiae, 1889). Weil on Homer, *Weil: An Anthology*, p. 194. Holst-Warhaft, *Dangerous Voices: Women's Laments and Greek Literature* (London, 1992), pp. 10–11. Don McCullin, *Unreasonable Behaviour: An Autobiography* (London, 1990), p. 214.

Chapter 9

Beckett, *Waiting for Godot* (1955), *Complete Dramatic Works* (London and Boston, 1986), p. 82. Pascal, *Pensées and Other Writings*, tr. Honor Levi (Oxford, 1995), p. 44. Middleton, *The Changeling*, V. iii. pp. 163–4, *Selected Plays*, ed. David L. Frost (Cambridge, 1978). *Catastrophe Survived: Euripides' Plays of Mixed Reversal*, by Anne Pippin Burnett (Oxford, 1971). Dennis quoted by Michelle Gellrich, *Tragedy and Theory: The Problem of Conflict since Aristotle* (Princeton, NJ, 1988), p. 216. Johnson on the death of Cordelia: *Johnson on Shakespeare*, ed. Arthur Sherbo, Yale Edition, vol. 8 (New Haven and London, 1968), p. 704. Abbé d'Aubignac, *La Pratique du théâtre* (1657), quoted by John D. Lyons, *Kingdom of Disorder: The Theory of Tragedy in Classical France* (West Lafayette, Indiana, 1999), p. xi. Strindberg, Preface to *Miss Julie* (1888), tr. Michael Meyer (London, 1964), pp. 92–3. Gorky, 'Fragments of Recollections' (1906), in *The Note-Books of Anton Chekhov*, tr. Koteliansky and Woolf, p. 107. 'Hegel's larger conception of history': Gellrich, *Tragedy and Theory*, p. 19. Bradley on Cordelia's death, *Shakespearean Tragedy* (1904), pp. 269–72; 'pain is mingled': 'Hegel's Theory of Tragedy' (1901), *Oxford Lectures on Poetry* (London, 1909), p. 84. Greensboro Truth and Community Reconciliation Project at *www.gtcrp.org*. Truth Commissions Digital Collection at *www.usip.org/library/truth.html*. St Paul, *Second Epistle to Timothy*, 4, 6; Wyclif and Rheims NT cited in *Oxford English Dictionary* under 'Resolution' (n.), definition 1. Aristotle: definition 3 of 'analysis' in *A Greek-English Lexicon* by Henry George Liddell and Robert Scott (Oxford, 1968), citing the *Nicomachean Ethics*, 1112^{b}23.

Further reading

General

John Drakakis and Naomi Conn Liebler (eds), *Tragedy*, Longman
Critical Reader (London, 1998); R. P. Draper (ed.), *Tragedy:
Developments in Criticism* (London, 1980).

Greek tragedy

P. E. Easterling (ed.), *The Cambridge Companion to Greek Tragedy*
(Cambridge, 1997); Simon Goldhill, *Reading Greek Tragedy*
(Cambridge, 1986); Rush Rehm, *Greek Tragic Theatre* (London, 1992);
Erich Segal (ed.), *Oxford Readings in Greek Tragedy* (Oxford, 1983);
M. S. Silk (ed.), *Tragedy and the Tragic: Greek Theatre and Beyond*
(Oxford, 1996); David Wiles, *Greek Theatre Performance: An
Introduction* (Cambridge, 2000).

Shakespeare and English Renaissance tragedy

D. F. Bratchell (ed.), *Shakespearean Tragedy* (London and New York,
1990); Stanley Cavell, *Disowning Knowledge in Seven Plays of
Shakespeare*, updated edn (Cambridge, 2003); Jonathan Dollimore,
*Radical Tragedy: Religion, Ideology and Power in the Drama of
Shakespeare and his Contemporaries*, 3rd edn (Basingstoke, 2004);
Richard Dutton and Jean E. Howard (eds), *A Companion to
Shakespeare's Works*, vol. I: *The Tragedies* (Oxford, 2003); Barbara
Everett, *Young Hamlet: Essays on Shakespeare's Tragedies* (Oxford,
1989); Susan Zimmerman (ed.), *Shakespeare's Tragedies* (Basingstoke,
1998).

Corneille and Racine

Roland Barthes, *On Racine*, tr. Richard Howard (New York, 1983); David Clarke, *Pierre Corneille: Poetics and Political Drama under Louis XIII* (Cambridge, 1992); Albert Cook, *French Tragedy: The Power of Enactment* (Chicago, 1981); Lucien Goldmann, *Racine*, tr. Alastair Hamilton (Cambridge, 1972); John D. Lyons, *Kingdom of Disorder: The Theory of Tragedy in Classical France* (West Lafayette, Indiana, 1999); Richard Parish, *Racine and the Limits of Tragedy* (Paris and Seattle, 1993).

Chapter 1

ORIGINS OF GREEK TRAGEDY: Gerald F. Else, *The Origin and Early Form of Greek Tragedy* (New York, 1965); John Herington, *Poetry into Drama: Early Tragedy and the Greek Poetic Tradition* (Berkeley, 1985); Richard Seaford, *Reciprocity and Ritual: Homer and Tragedy in the Developing City-State* (Oxford, 1994).

TRAGICOMEDY: Richard Dutton, *Modern Tragicomedy and the British Tradition* (Brighton, 1986); M. T. Herrick, *Tragicomedy: Its Origin and Development in Italy, France and England* (Urbana, 1962); D. L. Hirst, *Tragicomedy*, Critical Idiom Series (London and New York, 1984).

FORTUNE AND ACCIDENT: Henry Ansgar Kelly, *Chaucerian Tragedy* (Woodbridge, 1997); Ben Singer, *Melodrama and Modernity: Early Sensational Cinema and Its Contexts* (New York, 2001).

MODERN TRAGEDY: Terry Eagleton, *Sweet Violence: The Idea of the Tragic* (Oxford, 2003); Raymond Williams, *Modern Tragedy* (London, 1966; revised edn 1979).

ARISTOTLE: Stephen Halliwell, *Aristotle's Poetics* (London, 1986) and *The Poetics of Aristotle: Translation and Commentary* (London, 1987).

PLATO: excerpts from *Republic*, Book 2. 376 – Book 3. 398, and Book 10. 595–608, tr. D. A. Russell in *Ancient Literary Criticism*, eds D. A. Russell and M. Winterbottom (Oxford, 1972), pp. 50–74. Stephen

Halliwell, 'Plato's Repudiation of the Tragic', in Silk (ed.), *Tragedy and the Tragic*, pp. 332–50.

FEMINISM AND TRAGEDY: Linda Bamber, *Comic Women, Tragic Men: A Study of Gender and Genre in Shakespeare* (Stanford, 1982); Helene P. Foley, *Female Acts in Greek Tragedy* (Princeton, NJ, 2001); Coppélia Kahn, *Roman Shakespeare: Warriors, Wounds, and Women* (London, 1997); Nicole Loraux, *Tragic Ways of Killing a Woman*, tr. Anthony Forster (Cambridge, Mass., 1987).

TRAGIC EMOTIONS: Elizabeth S. Belfiore, *Tragic Pleasures: Aristotle on Plot and Emotion* (Princeton, NJ, 1992); A. D. Nuttall, *Why Does Tragedy Give Pleasure?* (Oxford, 1996); P[hilip] W[heelwright], 'Catharsis', in Alex Preminger (ed.), *Princeton Encyclopedia of Poetry and Poetics* (London and Basingstoke, 1975), pp. 106–8.

Chapter 2

STEINER: Ruth Padel, 'George Steiner and the Greekness of Tragedy', in Nathan A. Scott, Jr, and Ronald A. Sharp, *Reading George Steiner* (Baltimore and London, 1994), pp. 99–133; George Steiner, *The Death of Tragedy* (London, 1961; reprinted with new foreword, New York, 1980); *Antigones* (Oxford, 1984); 'A Note on Absolute Tragedy', *Journal of Literature and Theology*, 4(2) (July 1990): 147–56.

GREEK RELIGION: Walter Burkert, *Greek Religion* (Oxford, 1985); Mary Lefkowitz, *Greek Gods, Human Lives: What We Can Learn from Myths* (New Haven and London, 2003); Robert Parker, *Athenian Religion: A History* (Oxford, 1996).

CHRISTIANITY AND TRAGEDY: Lucien Goldmann, *The Hidden God: A Study of Tragic Vision in the 'Pensées' of Pascal and the Tragedies of Racine*, tr. Philip Thody (London, 1964); Karl Jaspers, *Tragedy Is Not Enough*, tr. Harold A. T. Reiche, Harry T. Moore, and Karl W. Deutsch (London, 1953); Richard B. Sewall, *The Vision of Tragedy* (New Haven, 1962; new edn 1980); Ulrich Simon, *Pity and Terror: Christianity and*

Tragedy (Basingstoke, 1989); Herbert Weisinger, *Tragedy and the Paradox of the Fortunate Fall* (London, 1953).

TRAGEDY AND MODERN DRAMA: Howard Barker, *Arguments for a Theatre*, 2nd edn (Manchester and New York, 1993); Arthur Miller, *Theatre Essays*, 2nd edn, ed. Robert A. Martin (London, 1994); John Orr, *Tragic Drama and Modern Society: A Sociology of Dramatic Form from 1880 to the Present*, 2nd edn (Basingstoke, 1989); Raymond Williams, *Drama from Ibsen to Brecht* (London, 1968).

Chapter 3

REVENGE: Anne Pippin Burnett, *Revenge in Attic and Later Tragedy* (Berkeley and London, 1998); John Kerrigan, *Revenge Tragedy: Aeschylus to Armageddon* (Oxford, 1996).

MOURNING: Margaret Alexiou, *The Ritual Lament in Greek Tradition* (Cambridge, 1974); Susan Cole, *The Absent One: Mourning Ritual, Tragedy, and the Performance of Ambivalence* (University Park, Pennsylvania, 1985); Heather Dubrow, *Shakespeare and Domestic Loss: Forms of Deprivation, Mourning, and Recuperation* (Cambridge, 1999); Sigmund Freud, 'Mourning and Melancholia' (1917), *Standard Edition of the Complete Psychological Works* (London, 1953–74), vol. 14; Gail Holst-Warhaft, *Dangerous Voices: Women's Laments and Greek Literature* (London, 1992); Olga Taxidou, *Tragedy, Modernity and Mourning* (Edinburgh, 2004).

HEROES: Reuben A. Brower, *Hero and Saint: Shakespeare and the Graeco-Roman Heroic Tradition* (New York, 1971); Bernard Knox, *The Heroic Temper: Studies in Sophoclean Tragedy* (Berkeley, 1964); Jean-Pierre Vernant and Pierre Vidal-Naquet, *Myth and Tragedy in Ancient Greece*, tr. Janet Lloyd (Cambridge, Mass., 1988).

PSYCHOLOGY AND PSYCHOANALYSIS: Philip Armstrong, *Shakespeare's Visual Regime: Tragedy, Psychoanalysis, and the Gaze* (Basingstoke, 2000); Sigmund Freud, *Art and Literature*, ed. Albert Dixon, The Pelican Freud Library, vol. 14 (Harmondsworth, 1985); Richard Kuhns,

Tragedy: Contradiction and Repression (Chicago, 1991); Ruth Padel, *In and Out of the Mind: Greek Images of the Tragic Self* (Princeton, NJ, 1992); Patrick Roberts, *The Psychology of Tragic Drama* (London and Boston, 1975); Bennett Simon, *Tragic Drama and the Family: Psychoanalytic Studies from Aeschylus to Beckett* (New Haven and London, 1988).

Chapter 4

OTHERS: Edith Hall, *Inventing the Barbarian: Greek Self-Definition through Tragedy* (Oxford, 1989).

GUILT AND SHAME: Friedrich Ohly, *The Damned and the Elect: Guilt in Western Culture* (Cambridge, 1992); Bernard Williams, *Shame and Necessity* (Berkeley and Oxford, 1993).

POLLUTION: Mary Douglas, *Purity and Danger: An Analysis of the Concepts of Pollution and Taboo* (London, 1966); Robert Parker, *Miasma: Pollution and Purification in Early Greek Religion* (Oxford, 1983).

SCAPEGOATS AND SACRIFICE: Helene P. Foley, *Ritual Irony: Poetry and Sacrifice in Euripides* (Ithaca, NY, 1985); René Girard, *Violence and the Sacred*, tr. Patrick Gregory (Baltimore, 1977), *The Scapegoat*, tr. Yvonne Freccero (Baltimore, 1986), and *A Theatre of Envy: William Shakespeare* (Oxford, 1991); Richard Gordon, 'Reason and Ritual in Greek Tragedy', *Comparative Criticism: A Yearbook*, 1, ed. Elinor Shaffer (Cambridge, 1979), pp. 279–310.

RITUAL: Rainer Friedrich, 'Drama and Ritual', in James Redmond (ed.), *Themes in Drama*, V: *Drama and Religion* (Cambridge, 1983), pp. 159–222; François Laroque, *Shakespeare's Festive World: Elizabethan Seasonal Entertainment and the Professional Stage*, tr. Janet Lloyd (Cambridge, 1991); Naomi Conn Liebler, *Shakespeare's Festive Tragedy: The Ritual Foundations of Genre* (London and New York, 1995).

Chapter 5

WAR: Philip Bobbitt, *The Shield of Achilles: War, Peace and the Course of History* (New York, 2002); Chris Hedges, *War Is a Force That Gives Us Meaning* (New York, 2002).

TRAGEDY AND PHILOSOPHY: Walter Kaufmann, *Tragedy and Philosophy* (Garden City, NY, 1969); Martha C. Nussbaum, *The Fragility of Goodness: Luck and Ethics in Greek Tragedy and Philosophy* (Cambridge, 1986; revised edn 2001).

TRAGEDY AND LITERARY THEORY: Stephen Booth, *King Lear, Macbeth, Indefinition, and Tragedy* (New Haven, 1983).

HEGEL: A. C. Bradley, 'Hegel's Theory of Tragedy', in *Oxford Lectures on Poetry* (London, 1909), pp. 69–98; Michelle Gellrich, *Tragedy and Theory: The Problem of Conflict since Aristotle* (Princeton, NJ, 1988); Robert Wicks, 'Hegel's Aesthetics: An Overview', in Frederick C. Beiser (ed.), *Cambridge Companion to Hegel* (Cambridge, 1993), pp. 348–77.

NIETZSCHE: Keith M. May, *Nietzsche and the Spirit of Tragedy* (Basingstoke, 1990); James I. Porter, *The Invention of Dionysus: An Essay on The Birth of Tragedy* (Stanford, 2000); M. S. Silk and J. P. Stern, *Nietzsche on Tragedy* (Cambridge, 1981).

MARSYAS: Edith Wyss, *The Myth of Apollo and Marsyas in the Art of the Italian Renaissance* (Cranbury, NJ, 1996).

PAIN: David B. Morris, *The Culture of Pain* (Berkeley and Los Angeles, 1991); Elaine Scarry, *The Body in Pain: The Making and Unmaking of the World* (New York and Oxford, 1985); Susan Sontag, *Regarding the Pain of Others* (London, 2003); Nigel Spivey, *Enduring Creation: Art, Pain and Fortitude* (London, 2001).

Chapter 6

COMEDY AND TRAGEDY: W. Kerr, *Tragedy and Comedy* (London, 1968); A. P. Rossiter, 'Comic Relief', in *Angel with Horns: Fifteen Lectures on*

Shakespeare, ed. Graham Storey (London, 1961; new edn 1989);
J. L. Styan, *The Dark Comedy*, revised edn (Cambridge, 1968).

SATYR PLAY: Richard Seaford, introduction to his edition of
Euripides' *Cyclops* (Oxford, 1984); Dana F. Sutton, 'The Satyr Play',
in P. E. Easterling and B. M. W. Knox (eds), *Cambridge History
of Classical Literature: Greek Literature* (Cambridge, 1985),
pp. 346–54.

REPETITION: Walter Benjamin, 'The Work of Art in the Age of
Mechanical Reproduction', *Illuminations*, ed. Hannah Arendt, tr. Harry
Zohn (London, 1970), pp. 219–54; Henri Bergson, *Le Rire* (1900), tr.
Cloudesley Brereton and Fred Rothwell as *Laughter: An Essay on the
Meaning of the Comic* (London, 1911); J. Hillis Miller, *Fiction and
Repetition: Seven English Novels* (Oxford, 1982).

Chapter 7

SENECA: A. J. Boyle, *Tragic Seneca: An Essay in the Theatrical Tradition*
(London, 1997); C. J. Herington, 'Senecan Tragedy', *Arion*, 5 (1966):
422–71; Charles Segal, 'Boundary Violation and the Landscape of the
Self in Senecan Tragedy', in *Interpreting Greek Tragedy: Myth, Poetry,
Text* (Ithaca and London, 1986), pp. 315–35.

SENECA'S INFLUENCE: Gordon Braden, *Renaissance Tragedy and the
Senecan Tradition: Anger's Privilege* (New Haven, 1985); T. S. Eliot,
'Shakespeare and the Stoicism of Seneca' (1927), in *Selected Essays*,
3rd edn (London, 1951); Robert S. Miola, *Shakespeare and Classical
Tragedy: The Influence of Seneca* (Oxford, 1992).

SILENCE IN SHAKESPEARE: Jean E. Howard, 'Speaking Silences on the
Shakespearean Stage', *Shakespeare's Art of Orchestration: Stage
Technique and Audience Response* (Urbana and Chicago, 1984); Philip
McGuire, *Speechless Dialect: Shakespeare's Open Silences* (Berkeley and
Los Angeles, 1985); Harvey Rovine, *Silence in Shakespeare: Drama,
Power, and Gender* (Ann Arbor and London, 1987).

SILENCE AND SPEECH: Tony Harrison, 'Facing up to the Muses' (1988), in *Tony Harrison*, Bloodaxe Critical Anthologies, ed. Neil Astley (Newcastle upon Tyne, 1991), pp. 429–54; Tillie Olsen, *Silences* (London, 1980); George Steiner, *Language and Silence* (London, 1967).

Chapter 8

TIME: T. F. Driver, *The Sense of History in Greek and Shakespearean Drama* (New York, 1960); David Scott Kastan, *Shakespeare and the Shapes of Time* (London, 1982); Frank Kermode, *The Sense of an Ending* (New York, 1967); Jacqueline de Romilly, *Time in Greek Tragedy* (Ithaca, NY, 1968); Wylie Sypher, *The Ethic of Time: Structures of Experience in Shakespeare* (New York, 1976).

RITES OF PASSAGE: Arnold van Gennep, *The Rites of Passage*, tr. Monika B. Vizedom and Gabrielle L. Caffe (London, 1960).

TRAGEDY IN THE VISUAL ARTS: Richard Green and Eric Handley, *Images of the Greek Theatre* (London, 1995); Jane Martineau (ed.), *Shakespeare in Art* (London, 2003); A. D. Trendall and T. B. L. Webster, *Illustrations of Greek Drama* (London, 1971).

PHOTOGRAPHY: Ken Light, *Witness in Our Time: Working Lives of Documentary Photographers* (Washington and London, 2000); Don McCullin, *Unreasonable Behaviour: An Autobiography* (London, 1990); John Taylor, *Body Horror: Photojournalism, Catastrophe and War* (Manchester, 1998).

Chapter 9

MELODRAMA: Michael Hays and Anastasia Nikolopoulou (eds), *Melodrama: The Cultural Emergence of a Genre* (Basingstoke, 1996); Robert Heilman, *Tragedy and Melodrama: Versions of Experience* (Seattle, 1968); James L. Smith, *Melodrama*, Critical Idiom Series (London, 1973).

ATTITUDES TO DEATH: Philippe Ariès, *Western Attitudes toward Death: From the Middle Ages to the Present*, tr. Patricia M. Ranum (Baltimore,

1974), and *The Hour of Our Death*, tr. Helen Weaver (London, 1981).

DYING: Fiona Macintosh, *Dying Acts: Death in Ancient Greek and Modern Irish Tragic Drama* (Cork, 1994); Michael Neill, *Issues of Death: Mortality and Identity in English Renaissance Tragedy* (Oxford, 1997); Christopher Ricks, *Beckett's Dying Words* (Oxford, 1993).

Tragedy

Index

Tragedy

Visit the
VERY SHORT
INTRODUCTIONS
Web site

www.oup.co.uk/vsi

➤ **Information** about all published titles

➤ News of **forthcoming books**

➤ **Extracts** from the books, including titles not yet published

➤ **Reviews** and views

➤ **Links** to other **web sites** and main OUP web page

➤ Information about **VSIs in translation**

➤ **Contact** the editors

➤ **Order** other **VSIs** on-line